MR. BAPTIST

JIMMY G. THARPE

21ST CENTURY
PRESS

SPRINGFIELD, MISSOURI 65807

MR. BAPTIST

ISBN 0-9728899-2-2

Cover: Lee Fredrickson
Book Design: Jeremy Montz and Terry White

Visit our web-site at: 21stcenturypress.com
                                and 21centurybooks.com

For childrens books visit: sonshippress.com
                                and sonshipbooks.com

21ST CENTURY
PRESS

PUBLISHING WITH PURPOSE

DEDICATION

First, I dedicate this book to my Heavenly Father who has made all things possible for me to enjoy my life, Mark 11:24.

I dedicate this book to my loving, supporting wife of 53 years, Edith Moore Tharpe. She worked so hard, under a short-term deadline, to put this all together for me.

I dedicate this book to my children and grandchildren who have added so much to my life.

I dedicate this book to the members of Trinity Baptist Church and Baptist Tabernacle who have loved me, prayed for me, and supported me throughout the years. Without them, I would be nothing.

I dedicate this book to the great host of friends and acquaintances I have loved so much and who have given me so much joy.

Special appreciation to my daughters, Kathy, Sharon, Debbye, Karen, and most of all my youngest daughter, Brenda who has worked day and night getting this book typed on the computer. Without them, I couldn't have completed this account of my life. Also, Don Edwards and Sam Vanni helped with the photographs and Loyd Cooper typed the first draft.

Finally this book is dedicated to all of YOU who have taken the time to read it and to Dr. Lee Fredrickson who has encouraged me to write my story.

TABLE OF CONTENTS

PROLOGUE

Mr. Baptist

One of the greatest compliments I ever received was the article "Mr. Baptist of Shreveport, Louisiana." On November 27, 1981, this article appeared in the headlines of the *Baptist Bible Tribune* written by Dr. Wendell Zimmerman, the editor. Dr. Zimmerman, who was truly a spiritual giant among fundamental Baptists, has gone on to be with the Lord, but I will always appreciate the confidence he placed in my ministry. This article is the foundation upon which this book is written. Excerpts from Dr. Zimmerman's tribute are as follows:

Many years ago, Shreveport was the home of a well known Baptist pastor, Dr. M.E. Dodd, pastor of the First Baptist Church of Shreveport. Dr. Dodd once served as president of the Southern Baptist Convention and because of his strong Baptist beliefs, he was known as "Mr. Baptist of Shreveport." His church sponsored Dodd College. He is now at home with the Lord.

Today, we have a new "Mr. Baptist of Shreveport," Dr. Jimmy Tharpe, who has been pastoring the Baptist Tabernacle for almost 27 years. I had the joy of sharing the pulpit of Baptist Tabernacle with Cecil Hodges in their annual Bible conference. Special music was provided by Mack Evans from Lynchburg, Virginia. It was a blessed time of fellowship and the preaching provided many blessings. Brother Tharpe and his large staff of workers were very gracious and it was a wonderful conference.

The ministry of J.G. Tharpe is absolutely outstanding. Baptist Tabernacle is solid and strong. The people have been well taught and they are real fundamental Baptists. In addition to the regular work of the church, the aggressive leadership has established many other ministries to reach and serve the community.

Tharpe has established Baptist Christian College for graduate studies and there is an enrollment of 117. In 1961 Baptist Christian College was founded. Today the college has state accreditation in Elementary Education, secondary social studies, and secondary physical education. There are 147 undergraduates enrolled and another 120 enrolled in a correspondence school.

Baptist Christian Academy was started in 1963. It begins with kindergarten and goes through 12th grade. The academy has an enrollment of 360. Kiddie Kollege, ages 2-4, has an enrollment of 30.

The above mentioned ministries were not sufficient to keep the preacher busy so he led the church in the establishment of the Baptist Christian Youth Encampment on a beautiful, 16 acre tract about 35 miles out of the city. The encampment is utilized by many other churches in the area.

The preacher evidently found a few spare moments, so the Baptist Christian Children's Home came into existence. Housed in a beautiful brick home near the church, there are currently 20 boys ages 9 through 17.

The church has extensive holdings in property providing sufficient room to expand all the ministries. The university and college are located on a 640 acre campus about 12 miles from the city. The 7 buildings were constructed for a public school but were taken over just this year by the Baptist Christian Schools. The 7 buildings are valued at 10 million dollars.

Brother Tharpe is a hard working pastor and aggressive leader. Mrs. Tharpe is well prepared and qualified to be an able assistant in the field of education. Every member of the staff, the teachers, the secretary, and the members were enthusiastic about past blessings, the present work, and the future prospects of the ministry of Baptist Tabernacle.

You can see why I felt so highly complimented and treasured every word of it. When I was giving my autobiography a title, this article came to mind, so you know how it came to be called "Mr. Baptist of Shreveport." At the end of this book there are 3 of my sermons which express my strong position on Baptist doctrine which I will hold until the Lord calls me home.

10

INTRODUCTION

They Call him "Mr. Baptist"

The call to be a pastor, a man of God, a spiritual leader is an awesome challenge. When the Holy Spirit lays a spiritual burden on the heart of a man, He intends to use him as an ambassador of Christ, a proclaimer of the gospel and a teacher of truth.

Remember that God told Jeremiah that he had been selected before he was even born (Jeremiah 1:5). His long and faithful ministry and powerful preaching covered the last decades of spiritually decadent Judah before the Babylonian conquests (606 and 586 B.C.) and the destruction of Jerusalem . . . and beyond.

He experienced great triumphs and severe hardships, yet remained loyal to the Lord always, rising spiritually from discouragement during periods of persecution. No prophet was more revered by the ancient Jews who lived before the coming of Christ.

Jeremiah's greatest contribution was his written book...even now it is being read all around the world some 2500 years after his death. His long shadow of influence remains intact through the inspired writings of his life, and through those who were encouraged by his faith.

The same is true for many spiritual leaders and preachers and writers today.

In our times, Jimmy G. Tharpe has likewise cast a long and enduring shadow for good and will until Jesus comes.

Here we will lovingly and candidly look into his life and work. This book is a serious, and yet entertaining, account of a ministry that spanned over half a century.

Saved at the age of twenty in 1951, Jimmy began his ministry as a Methodist. The following year, while studiously reading the Bible and praying for divine guidance, he was convicted to become a Baptist. That same year he then founded his first church, the Trinity Baptist Church of Doyline, Louisiana, which he pastored until 1956.

Moving to Shreveport later that year, he began his lifetime work at Baptist Tabernacle on Hollywood Avenue and saw it quickly grow in those early days. During the 1950s he both pastored and continued his educational pursuits, earning first a bachelor's degree at Louisiana Baptist Institute and Seminary. Later he finished B.A. and M.A. degrees from Trinity College in Florida, also accumulating many credits at Centenary College in Shreveport and East Texas Baptist College in Marshall for later transfer to Trinity. He completed his PH.D at National Christian University.

As he studied the Word, growing in fellowship and faith, while winning souls and building a great church, young Jimmy Tharpe also caught the vision of God's desire for the training of pastors, missionaries and laypeople for Christian ministries all over the world.

His roots were in the "Landmark Baptist" branch of the Baptist movement, which arose in the 19th century and was led by such great leaders and theologians as James R. Graves, and later by Ben M. Bogard. Jimmy's steadfast convictions as a Baptist have characterized his life and ministry, yet he has reached out to help other servants of the Lord in the great Family of God, particularly in the realm of education.

In 1961 he founded Baptist Christian College and three years later he founded Baptist Christian Academy. This led into the organization of a 4-year resident college in Shreveport which operated for many years.

It was in 1973, however, that Baptist Christian University was inaugurated to help those pastors, evangelists, missionaries and others who couldn't leave their home or mission field to engage in continuing education. Baptist Christian University met their need for long-distance learning. In 1988 Louisiana Baptist Theological Seminary was incorporated with this writer as first president.

He was a pioneer in what is now the fastest growing method of education in America, non-traditional distance learning.

Baptist Christian University, now known as Louisiana Baptist University and Theological Seminary, has enrolled and graduated thousands of distance learning students.

The Baptist Tabernacle has also reached thousands of people through her decades in Shreveport, and additionally sponsored, launched or assisted dozens of other new churches, mostly in the southern states, as home mission projects and extensions.

The high point of attendance at the 11 acre campus of the Baptist Tabernacle was reached in the early 1980s, when a special all day Sunday School rally attracted over 6000 people.

Widely known as an evangelist and special guest preacher,

Jimmy Tharpe has spoken in literally hundreds of churches, large and small, over a 50-year ministry. Various schools with honorary doctoral degrees have honored him, including Tennessee Temple University in Chattanooga, Midwestern Baptist College in Pontiac, Michigan, Landmark Baptist College, and Bradford Academy.

As he ministered to so many, he also became many things to many people. Some comment on his powerful preaching ministry; others remember a mission he established; some will cherish the memory of his tender loving care for them as they went through dark trials and serious tragedies; many look to him as a great patriarch and Baptist leader. The Preacher is many things to many, impacting thousands overtime.

So what shall we more say?

Here is the life story of a great preacher, a defender of the faith, a classical Baptist loyalist, a pioneering educator, a compassionate pastor, a friend of preachers, a motivator of men and women to serve God more effectively, an example of godliness, a dynamic leader with both courage and humility, a good husband and father . . . and much more. Thus it is, he is not alone.

Constantly supporting, inspiring and encouraging him is one of the great women I have known. Edith Tharpe, co-worker, team leader and great educator in her own right (she earned a Doctor of Education degree from Northwestern State University at Natchitoches Louisiana) has been at his side.

They have always served as a team.

Through these printed pages, step now into their lives. Smile, laugh, admire and enjoy this real story of real people in real life situations in the service of the Lord.

The impact of this ministry lives on in the men and women, young and old, and the young people who have heard him preach and teach, in the lives of those who attended his church, studied in schools he launched, worked with him in home and foreign missionary enterprises and have known and loved him.

We honor our dear friend and colleague, Jimmy G. Tharpe "Mr. Baptist," whose leadership and influence will continue now and until Jesus comes. Read on!

—James O. Combs

I have always been an optimist and believed in the power of positive thinking. There were two men in jail with different views. When they looked through the bars, one saw the mud, the other saw the stars.

CHAPTER 1

EARLY DAYS AND FAMILY

In the small town of Sibley, Louisiana, nothing much exciting ever happened. Life was simple and living was carefree and easy. Probably the key fact and source of entertainment for the town was that 31 of its citizens were alcoholics. (Another older, more descriptive word for this is "drunks".)

To the Tharpe family, the town of Sibley and Bayou Dorcheat were magical. It may be that one of the founding families, George and Molly Tharpe, raised their children here, who later raised their children, and on and on. My wife, Edith, designed a family tree that shows all the descendants of this couple who surely didn't realize what they had started. My brother, Jack, will not be caught outside the city limits when darkness falls if at all possible. He loves Sibley very much and has never lived anywhere else in his life.

On May 12, 1930, there was an exception to the rule about excitement in Sibley. A baby boy was added to the L.H. and Fern Tharpe family. The first child, Bonnie Lee, had passed away when she was eight years old with malaria. Jimmy Gid Tharpe was the first born son and much loved by his parents. God later added two more boys, George Norman and Jack Donald to complete the Tharpe family.

My birthday was a special day according to my mother who loved to tell the story. A strange phenomenon occurred when I arrived with a veil over my face. According to my mother this meant I was a special person in some way because this was a rare occurrence. When God called me to preach in 1951 this was His explanation for the veil, since there is no higher calling than to be a preacher and minister of God.

Many times when my brothers and I are together we find ourselves reflecting on the many blessings of our humble beginning. Our house was very small, consisting of three rooms and a "path" with no electricity. We cut stove wood for an old pot bellied stove on which my mother cooked many delicious meals.

It was a wonderful blessing when we got electricity and we enjoyed this convenience very much. Our home was blessed with a sweet Christian mother. I can almost hear her singing now, "What A Friend We Have In Jesus" as she went about doing her daily chores for our little family. My mother could take a few items such as a little corn meal and a few lima beans and prepare a meal for us kids. Of course, this was in the days of the Great Depression and no one had very much.

My father made our living as a fisherman. I remember so many times he would come in bringing fish and wild game to cook. We thought we were rich. Many times his boat would be filled with squirrels, plenty of good game fish, and maybe a duck or two that he had shot on the wing. With a dozen traps, he might have a coon and every now and then a mink.

We would seine crawfish when we got out of school and he would bait his troutlines with them. His equipment consisted of a couple of troutlines, two wire nets, sometimes one hoop net, a cane pole that he used to catch bass, and a single barrel shotgun.

This meager equipment enabled my father to provide for us, and he loved this type of life. He was surely the luckiest fisherman I ever knew. I remember once when he came in with a big buffalo fish and a smaller one. My father knew I was a big eater and he said to Mr. Cantrell, our next door neighbor, "This big fish is for Jimmy, and the small one is for the rest of the family." We all had a good laugh because even then I wasn't shy about eating.

We had a lot of happiness in our little home and we often look back on the good times. We had a milk cow named Jane for a number of years. We also had a good garden and, even though we didn't have much money, had plenty to eat and never missed a meal.

The day came when old Jane died and I shall never forget

that sad afternoon. I came home from school, my mother was weeping and said, "What will we do?" We all agreed that we should trust in the Lord and keep on keeping on.

In my mind's eye, I can still see my youngest brother, Jack, standing on the porch, waiting until Mama came in with a bucket of milk. Before she could strain it, he would beg for hot milk. She'd say, "Wait until I strain it, son." He would stand and cry until she poured him a hot glass of milk. He still likes warm milk to this day.

I also remember many things about my brother, George. He was always building something and very talented in doing so. He would sometimes hire himself out to have some spending money. One of his jobs was to go to Mrs. Liddy Boyd's store for Aunt Nellie, and she would pay him two pennies. I had a vision to contract George's services, pay him one penny and keep the other for myself. This worked very well until he caught on and stopped my vision in its tracks.

The Tharpe's have always been well known for their wit and quick answers. They love to make people laugh, and to scare someone is even better.

I remember bath time as a child. We waited until after dark because we had to bathe outside on the porch. I took pleasure in crawling under the house while my brothers took their bath, jumping out, and giving them both a good scare. The result was usually that someone ran screaming through the house unclad.

That was my idea of great fun because I have always been

a big joker, but I have learned to watch over that characteristic, lest I become a practical joker.

When I was in my early years at school, I came to realize that maybe we weren't so rich after all. At lunchtime we would all take what we brought from home and go out to the schoolyard and eat under the big tree. I usually sat beside the Braswell brothers. They were from one of the wealthier families in Sibley and I liked to sit beside them to listen to the interesting stories they told.

My mother would pack our sack lunches every morning which usually consisted of biscuits with egg inside or some type of jelly. I watched daily as the Braswell boys unfolded their nice, light bread sandwiches, and longed for the day that we could have light bread in our lunch sacks. As a result of knowing I would be taking biscuits from my sack, I often hid behind the tree to eat so no one would see what I was having for lunch. I chuckle about this now. What would the man of today give for a sack of my mother's biscuits for any meal?

One day I happened to get the wrong lunch. When the sacks were passed out, I was handed a sack with light bread. I suspected something wasn't quite right but I chose for the moment to ignore it. I quickly stepped into the crowd of students so everyone would see me open a light bread sandwich for the first time. It was beautifully wrapped in cellophane, something else I had not yet had the pleasure of seeing in my sack.

At that very moment I heard the shrill voice of my teacher, Mrs. Sutton, yelling out, "Jimmy! I think you might have the wrong lunch." She walked over to me and said, "Oh yes, here is your lunch," and presented me with my sack of biscuits. I knew it was my lunch because I could see the grease seeping through the sack. She then presented the Braswell boy his lunch that was handed to me by mistake, and everyone knew that Jimmy had biscuits.

That day, for the first time, I ate them without shame in front of everyone. I had been caught with the light bread and as the Bible says, "Be sure your sins will find you out." What my teacher knew then, and I know now, is that being poor wasn't a shame. The biscuits in my sack were the best lunch my humble mother could prepare.

God blessed me with many friends in my younger years even though I had not yet followed Christ. I was well loved and have always been a lover of people.

I was fortunate enough to meet two of the best friends I ever had when I was a young boy, Harry Smith and Leon Snyder. Mother was certain that any mischief I got into was the entire fault of one of these two boys. I was quick to agree with her, even though we three boys have always known this was not necessarily the case.

We three did a large variety of things together year after year...riding freight trains, camping, and playing sports together. In 1946, we represented Sibley High School in the State Championship. We lost the game to Doyline High School, but defended our honor one-week later by beating them in a tournament. Harry and Leon remain close friends until this day.

My times at Sibley High were some of the best in my life. I graduated in eleven years at the age of sixteen. There were only seven in my graduating class and I often teased them by saying I would be at the top of the list of good grades if you turned the list upside down. Still, it was noteworthy to graduate from high school in those years. Many students were forced to quit school and go to work to support their families.

The "Sibley Bridge" was the main gathering place for the boys during the day and late at night. The Illinois Central Depot was the meeting place for all the young people at 5 p.m. when the train came through. That gives you an idea of how much there was to do in our small town. Nobody had a car, so we had to walk everywhere we went and we went where we thought we might see the most action. We all knew that if you come and go out of Sibley, you will go by way of the "Bridge."

It was quite an honor for me to be both Senior Class President on the serious side and "Class Clown" on the lighter side. I thought it was my job to keep everyone laughing. My mother often said, "Ole Jim loves to be the center of attention. If he's at the wedding he wants to be the bride, and if he's at the funeral he wants to be the corpse." She knew me very well.

These are some of the sweetest memories in my life because of great friends and family. I love them more than words can express.

It was my sweet privilege at the age of seventeen to go to work for the railroad and be able to assist in sending my younger brothers to school. I can remember on payday I would give my mother my check. I would only hold back ten dollars to live on.

Sometimes I had to borrow money, twenty-five cents interest on a dollar. I would get behind but always managed to overcome it. It was important to me that Mama and the family did not suffer.

At the time my father was drinking heavily. He knew I would do my best to see that the family was taken care of, and that seemed to make him a little less concerned. When my father would drink it would break my heart as well as the other boys. He was a good father and we loved him dearly, but his biggest problem was drinking.

I remember the night I received a Masters Degree from the Masonic Order. I looked out the window and saw the jail where I had to have my own father locked up. This was heartbreaking, but it was the right thing to do since he had gotten into a fight with his brother. I got them out of jail the next day. "You did what you should have done," they said.

My father used to say he would own half of Webster Parish had he not been a drinking man. I have no doubt he was telling the truth.

He was an extremely talented man, and well loved by everyone who knew him. His nickname was Smokey, and he is still referred to by that name today. I believe Daddy blamed God for taking Bonnie at such a tender age. Sometimes, while under the influence, he would say, "If God is such a gracious God, how could He take little Bonnie?"

I heard that for years. Finally I heard it one too many times. I said one of the hardest things I ever said to my father that day. "I don't know why God does some things Daddy, but I think one reason he might have taken Bonnie is that you were not fit to raise her."

Daddy never would come hear me preach until shortly after I made that statement about Bonnie. I think this helped to lead him to come for the first time. He sat through the service, and during the invitation he ran down the aisle, grabbed me around the neck, and said, "Jim, I want to be saved."

We prayed together and my father asked Christ to come into his heart. I really believe my father was saved that day, but for years he doubted his salvation. I believe he had a lot of guilt because of the lifestyle he led for so many years. He asked the Lord to save him two more times after that night.

"Saved by works" had been instilled in him as a young boy, and he always wanted to make sure he was going to Heaven.

Shortly after my mother died he was baptized at Sibley Missionary Baptist. He came to me that night fearing he was lost. Again we got down and prayed and he asked Christ to come into his heart. The last time was shortly before he died. He attended a service at Baptist Tabernacle, got down on his knees at the altar, and asked God to save him again.

My father fought the "battle of the bottle." For many months he would be clear of drink. He would attend church with my mother at Trinity. These times were great and everyone was happy. Then came the periods where he would go back on the bottle.

I don't know how to explain this, but I do know John 5:24 tells us, "He that heareth my word and believeth on Him that sent me hath everlasting life and shall not come into condemnation, but is passed from death unto life." I have the assurance I will see my father in Glory. I long for that day.

Courtship and Marriage

Fishing, camping, and hunting have always been a very important part of my life and for a long time my number one interest. Then the desire came, as with all young boys, to start thinking of the girls. While enlisted in the National Guard at Camp Beauregard in Alexandria, Louisiana, I received a letter from a friend. He informed me that two pretty girls had moved to Sibley. Their father, Mr. Martin Moore, was an engineer with the railroad. It was always a big thing for pretty girls to move to a little town. I wrote back and said, "Have a good time now fellows, because I plan to take over when I get home."

The first time I met Edith Moore, she was walking across the Sibley Bridge to go to the First Baptist Church. Several of us were on our way to go swimming. I told her who I was and asked her if she would like to go swimming. She said, "No, thank you, I go to church on Sunday."

She was dressed in a white dress, and that day is one I will never forget. I said, "You can go to church when you can't go anywhere else." She replied sweetly, "I always go to church on Sunday." She then walked right across the bridge and continued on her way to church. Of course, my buddies horse-laughed me, and rightly so. But I knew that very day that Edith was the one for me. I even told the boys, "That will be my wife." That gave them another good laugh, but for me it was love at first sight.

When I first visited her home, I was unaware of the fact she had already met one of the Tharpe boys. My younger brother, George, had run over her on his bicycle, knocking her into a ditch. She laughed about it then and still laughs about it today.

I went to see her for thirty-one nights straight. I was hanging around so much that Mrs. Moore could not pour dishwater out without hitting me in the head. I liked to think I was the only person she wanted to date, but the truth was no one else had the opportunity to date her with me at her doorstep for a solid month. She would later prove to my heart that it truly was love at first sight by saying, "I will."

There were times when I would go to church with Edith because I had to attend church in order to date her. This proved to be a tremendous blessing for me. Later, because of her sweet testimony, I was drawn under conviction to become a Christian.

We often kid, and this is true, that I never asked Edith to marry me. We loved one another so much we simply assumed it would come to pass. Still, I will always regret the fact that I never asked her father for her hand in marriage.

In the 1948-49 Sibley High School Yearbook, an interesting preview of our lives is written. The class prophecy stated that the Reverend and Mrs. Jimmy Tharpe were pastoring a church. This prediction was supposed to be as far from reality as possible. It brought a lot of laughter to the readers. I was as far from a preacher as the north is from the south. About five years later this became a reality. Actually, God was beginning to bring His plan for Edith and me to the minds of family and friends long before we knew it ourselves.

We were happily married on April 21, 1950. Our honeymoon consisted of the short trip from Buck Hall to our new house where we would spend our first weekend as man and wife. Many of our dear friends, under the influence of my lifelong friends Harry and Leon, decided to spend the night with us and did exactly that. We sat up all night long. Around midnight, Edith cooked steak with rice and gravy, and everyone had a big meal. We all had a wonderful time.

I believe at the time they were trying to see if we would try to get rid of them. In the end, the joke was on them because they helped to make our honeymoon night a unique one we have fondly remembered over the years.

Four months later Harry Smith and Lou McCabe were married. We all took a honeymoon trip to New Orleans, Louisiana, and had a wonderful time together. A big trip like this was not something people from Sibley often experienced. It made up for the original "unique" honeymoon night.

Edith was always faithful in church, and wanted us to worship together as a family. She had set this pattern for herself years earlier while living in New Orleans. She attended church faithfully, often times going alone. She witnessed to me in many ways, most of all by her consistent Christian life. I often credit my own salvation to her being the Christian leader in the early years of our marriage. The few times I had gone to church in my life were mostly times that I went to be by her side.

She gradually lost interest in going to church early in the marriage. We had a little schedule we followed. I played ball on Sibley's Town Team and the games were on Sunday afternoon. After the game we would eat out and go to a movie. We both enjoyed this lifestyle and had many good times with our friends.

When we were expecting our first child, Edith received a heavy conviction about her church attendance. She felt that if she did not serve God, something would surely happen to our baby. She began to ask me to go to church with her on Sunday morning. I was reluctant to attend the Baptist Church, so instead she agreed to go to the Methodist Church with me.

One Saturday afternoon, we decided to attend my church the following morning. My dad came to visit late that afternoon and said, "Jim, a "Blue Norther" is coming in and the ducks are moving. We need to go hunting in the morning." Edith said, "Oh, no! He has already promised to go to church with me!"

As any young, macho man would do, I chose to go hunting so that no one would think of me as henpecked. This really hurt Edith and she started to cry. My mother said, "Don't cry, Edith, I will go to church with you." They began to go to the Methodist Church together and Edith did not mention church to me again.

A while passed, and I decided maybe I should go to church and I began to attend on Sunday morning. Since duck season was over I figured it would be a good time to grace them with my presence. As Strange as it was at the time, I began to enjoy the services. There was more involved than I knew, as God was working His plan in my life.

CHAPTER 2

SALVATION AND CALL TO PREACH

There was one particular church service at Sibley Methodist Church that I remember well. Brother L.M. Sawyer preached a sermon called "Under The Blood." I was convicted as I sat listening and I knew I needed to accept Christ as my personal Savior. I made my way down that little Methodist aisle, fell on my knees, and asked Jesus to come into my heart.

He saved my soul and I felt as light as a feather. My life was changed at that moment. It was a red-letter day for me as it is for all people. I spent the following days rejoicing and I turned my life over to God's will. Even though I knew little about the Bible, I was soon teaching a class. I remember the first time I prayed in public. I actually called on myself to pray. Having very little knowledge of the Word of God, I even had Kathy christened as a baby because at the time, I did not understand the scripture.

I took the young people as my project and more of them began attending church. One of the converts was Lila Ann Hillidge. Little did I know that she would later become my sister-in-law by marrying my brother George.

I knew my life was on track and I was in the will of God for the first time in my life. I never thought about where the road would end, I just knew I had to be on the road. I wanted that more than anything.

I began to grow in grace through reading and studying God's word. The more I studied the more I wanted to learn.

For years I had played baseball on Sunday. Once, after a Sunday game, I was sitting in a little restaurant. I looked across the way at some people filing into church for evening worship and knew that, as a saved person, I should not play ball on Sunday. I turned my suit in to the team the next day. Some of the players said they would save my suit for me because I would be back, but I never went back to get it. I was now playing in the big leagues for Christ and nothing but His will seemed to matter in my life. I became concerned about God's will for my life and began to pray for His direction.

At the time I did not understand how God called a man to preach. When I heard Brother Sawyer preach, it seemed that God put the belief in my heart that He wanted me to preach. This stayed with me for days.

One day I asked Pastor Sawyer if he would like to go squirrel hunting with me. We headed to Bayou Dorcheat and when we arrived I sat down, leaned my shotgun on a log, and said, "I really didn't come here to go hunting, but to discuss something dear to my heart." He said, "What is it, Jimmy?" I said, "I feel like God wants me to preach and I don't know how to begin." I asked him how he arrived at his decision to preach the gospel. We talked for a long time and I asked him for the opportunity, on the day of his choosing, to allow me to preach in the church.

That day came, and he suddenly announced that I would be preaching in the evening service. I was happy but worried because I knew nothing about sermon preparation or homiletics. These things were foreign to me.

I went home that afternoon with a little notebook. I pulled the shades down, and got down on my knees and asked God to help me prepare a sermon.

I knew very little about the Bible and did not know where to start. I came across a passage of scripture in Matthew that referred to God being able to aid the children of Abraham. I said in my heart, this will be my sermon, "God Is Able." I asked the Lord for the ability to be able to preach with power.

God moved in that service and several people were saved. One young man who received Christ was a second cousin, Tommy O'Rear. From that night forward, I knew God had put His hand on me to preach the wonderful riches of the Bible. I had invited some of the ball players that had been my friends for many years. They were all sitting in the back of the church. This was a new adventure for me and I was fearful.

I was licensed to preach in the Methodist Conference in Ruston, Louisiana, in a ceremony attended by the officials of the Methodist Church, Brother and Mrs. Sawyer, Edith and me. One of the requirements of the Methodist Church was that I agree never to smoke. I left there thinking I was now a big preacher and ready for anything. They suggested it would be necessary for Edith to become a Methodist.

After much persuasion she reluctantly gave in and joined, but it was not according to her wishes. On the way home from the licensing ceremony, Brother Sawyer lit a cigarette. I asked him why he could smoke and I could not. He said, "I am a shell-shocked veteran and the doctor wrote a letter to excuse me from that rule." I saw that as a green light to continue smoking myself. I asked Brother Sawyer for his doctor's name. I needed a letter myself.

In the Methodist denomination they had what were called "charges." I had opportunities to preach at these different churches. In the absence of the pastor, I was allowed to fill in. There were no Sunday night services at the time, and I asked the preacher if we could begin to have them. He said, "Yes, if you would like to preach we will have them." I gladly accepted.

I wanted to be preaching the gospel. Sometimes I would get in my car and drive to other "charges." One of these was at Pine Grove Methodist, where the Methodists worshiped one Sunday and the Baptists worshiped the next.

Some folks began to reason with me about denominational issues. My wife and her people were staunch Missionary

Baptist and would not come to hear me preach. Finally, my wife asked one of her uncles to come and hear me preach even though this was a big no-no for their family.

Her Uncle Albert came and that night I preached on the subject, "The Woman at the Well." In my sermon I stated, "If you drink of this water you shall never thirst." After the service he said, "Jimmy, they will kick you out of this church." I asked why and he informed me I was preaching Baptist doctrine. I said, "Uncle Albert, I am just preaching the Bible." He looked at me as if to say, "I know some things you don't, Sonny." Later on I found out what he meant.

Approximately six months had passed by then and in this period of time my brother-in-law, Albert Moore, invited me to attend services with him in Minden, Louisiana. We were going to hear an evangelist named Foster Lott who was preaching a tent revival nightly and going great guns. I accepted and Albert and I attended the meeting. That night Albert was saved and it made me very happy.

Brother Foster Lott was a missionary out of Calvary Missionary Baptist Church where he held membership. After the services I approached Brother Lott. "We sure enjoyed your message, and I am so happy Albert was saved," I said to this man of God. "I would like for you to come to Sibley. We need a revival and I think we may be missing something your message would bring to us."

He said, "Do you know what you are asking me to do?" I said, "Yes sir, I want you to come to Sibley, put your tent up, and preach in my hometown the way I heard you preach here tonight." "I'll pray about it," he replied. He often chewed gum, and was chewing it at that moment with a pleasant smile on his face. I will never forget that night.

One day he arrived in Sibley with his tent and his helpers. Together we were all working to get the big tent up. We worked hard and I was very excited. Edith's mother, Ruth Moore, prepared a great dinner for us. I was enjoying the meal until I heard a horn blow in the front yard.

I walked out into the yard and saw two people sitting in the car, Brother Sawyer, pastor of the United Methodist Church, and one of his members. He said, "Jimmy, are you aware that we have a board meeting at the church, and as Superintendent of Sunday School you are required to be there?" I explained that I was aware of the meeting but did not know I was required to attend.

I apologized to him and explained that I was helping Brother Lott pitch the tent to hold the revival meeting in Sibley. It made him angry and he said, "If you're going to have a revival meeting, don't go with some fly-by-night Baptist preacher." I highly resented his statement. He said a few more words and quickly drove away.

I have never understood all the works of Satan, but I do know that conversation was a great disappointment for me. We went on and the tent revival got underway. Brother Lott preached in a sport shirt. I remember he preached so hard and in one illustration said, "Some people have tongues so long, they can sit in the living room and lick a skillet in the kitchen." I thought this was so funny and very true.

It so happened that there was a gossiper near by who heard this, and spread it all over town. News was flashing everywhere about the big meeting. I began to pray that God would show me what to do.

I had studied enough doctrine to believe the doctrine of eternal security of the saved as well as the other articles of the Baptist faith and I knew I believed it with all of my heart. My wife had conveniently left a *Baptist Way Book* by Ben Bogard lying on the table, and I read it when I was alone. I was thoroughly convinced God was leading me to become a Baptist.

At times I became angry with those who wanted me to be a Baptist and I would lash out at them because I thought they believed that if you were not a Baptist you would not go to Heaven. We all know this is not true and that only the blood of Christ saves us.

When I revealed my new convictions to Edith, I asked her to go with me to visit Brother Sawyer. I had my scriptures underlined to show him the glorious doctrine of "Once Saved Always Saved." I was fearful when we entered the door. I explained to him that God had led me to join the Baptist church. I asked him to pray for me and explained that I wanted to show him why. I opened my Bible and said, "I want to show you the scriptures."

He fell on his knees, grabbed my legs, and said, "Jimmy, you can't do this. This is not right." He wept so hard it touched my heart. Then Mrs. Sawyer said, "After all we have done for you, you are going to desert the Methodist church and leave us as well?" Then she told me that an "ungrateful friend is worse than a jagged tooth, or a broken bone."

I could not contain myself and I began to weep. This meeting did not go anything like I had planned. I ended up in the study of the parsonage weeping convulsively and unable to contain myself. I remember seeing my brother-in-law, Ed Boyd, and my sister-in-law, Norma, getting out of the car. They had come to take me to Minden Hospital where I spent four days. They called it a nervous breakdown. I don't know how nerves break down, but I knew something had gone terribly wrong.

They allowed no visitors at all, but somehow Brother Lott slipped in. He was chewing his gum as he usually did. He said, "Jim, it is the devil fighting your ministry. It is going to be all right, and I want you to know I am praying for you. God is preparing you for later things." His visit meant so much to my heart.

Another visitor arrived soon after. Brother M.L. Davis, a man who loved us dearly, and had performed the ceremony when Edith and I were married. He said, "Jimmy, I started to become a Baptist once myself. If you want to be a Baptist it's all right. I can assure you of that. But you need to go with the Southern Baptist Convention where you can be promoted and have better opportunities."

I did not follow this advice, as you will later read. Then Dr. Cook, who had delivered Kathy, came in. "Now Jimmy, I'm a religious man (and he used an ugly word), but you're taking this too seriously. You really need to stop and understand. You have a good job with the railroad, and you will not do your family any good if you end up in the state hospital." This was more discouragement, and at this point I was so frustrated, I did not know what to do.

I came home from the hospital and my loved ones had raised fifty dollars, which was a week's salary in those days. They gave this to me with a sweet letter saying how much they loved me and how they wanted me to stay with the Methodist Church. Another lady, whose name I will not mention, wrote me a letter and said, "If you don't apologize to Brother Sawyer and get back into the Methodist Church, God will take Kathy." I wondered if this could be a special message from God. I was afraid and began to weep.

My wife had suspicions of the letter's origin, and took it to the Methodist Church and checked the handwriting. She then knew who it was, though she had already guessed. At that time I made up my mind that I was quitting the ministry and would never preach again.

I had quit for approximately a week when one night Edith woke me up and said, "Get up quickly, I think Kathy is dead." I said, "No, not Kathy, not my baby." We wrapped her in a blanket and jumped into the car to head for the hospital. She was suffering from an extremely high fever. I was praying and weeping.

When we arrived at the hospital they began to work on Kathy. They packed her in ice. I found a solitary place where I could pray that God would spare my child. He did, and the next day the doctor informed us that she was going to be fine. They didn't know what was wrong with her, but I did. I knew it was a warning from God. I made God a promise that I would never stop preaching.

Brother Lott, a Baptist preacher, took me, a Methodist, on soul-winning visitation one day. We visited my first cousin, Alys Ruth McLemore, who is like a sister to me. Brother Lott went through the plan of salvation as I watched. Alys was gloriously saved and I had my first experience of seeing the "New Birth" first hand.

Since that day I have loved winning souls and try to practice it at every opportunity. Brother Lott's wife, Nancy, was a perfect example to all the young preacher's wives. She also was a soul-winner and reminded me of the woman the Bible refers to in Proverbs 31.

I began to follow the Bible's advice on moving ahead for the Lord. In Philippians 3:13-14 it states, "Forgetting those things which are behind and reaching forward to those things which are ahead, I press toward the mark for the prize of the high calling of God in Christ Jesus."

Before I had time to recuperate I was in attendance at Calvary Baptist Church in Minden, Louisiana, where I joined and was baptized. I told Brother Clover when I went down the aisle that I wanted to move my letter. He laughed and told me that I had never been baptized scripturally and did not have a letter to move. At this church I was introduced to some major Baptist policies.

My wife, however, did have a letter to move and was very happy to do so.

A week later, Brother Lott had enlisted me in his mission

church in Doyline, Louisiana, where my life in the "real" ministry began. The church met in a storefront building with only five people in attendance the first Sunday. It was June and extremely hot but God continued to bless. Soon we were off and running to build Trinity Baptist Church.

Most people would say that I have a strange philosophy of life. I had rather shoot big and miss than never to shoot at all.

CHAPTER 3

TRINITY BAPTIST CHURCH

Trinity Baptist Church had a very humble beginning. The five people we started with took responsibility to grow the church and soon we had enough to start a building for worship. But keep in mind that the church was at a serious disadvantage since their pastor was a converted Methodist and green as a gourd. I had so much to learn about Baptists and they were my teachers!

We bought one acre of land and I set out to clear it. All I had was a hoe with a broken handle and the weeds were almost waist high. I was attempting to cut the tall weeds when a man whose name I cannot recall, came up and asked, "What are you doing, Preacher?" I told him I was starting to build a church.

He asked what he could do to help. I said, "I need a pole so we can have an electrical hookup. This is where our church will be built." On that little act of faith, God blessed, and there was no end to the work that was done there in four years as pastor of those wonderful people.

The church people began to pray and God heard and answered. The people of Doyline were mostly kind, loving, and gentle people who only wanted a nice place to worship God. The other Baptist Church was a little bit snobbish and some of their folks poked fun at us as we worshiped in the storefront building.

At school, our young people were teased about where we taught the boys and girls. The shelves of the store were still marked Boys Department and Girls Department. We tried to get them out of there as soon as possible to save them further embarrassment.

We had no money to build but we had plenty of determination. I heard of a man by the name of Milton Lambert who helped to build churches in that area. I contacted Mr. Lambert and he was so gracious. He owned a lumber and building materials company where he financed construction projects. His interest rates were high but that was not a concern to us because he said, "I will let you have the materials on credit and bill you for it."

Because of my age, I was unafraid of debt. I used to say things like, "Let's owe a million more in '84." Since I am older, I realize what a burden debt can be.

Soon he delivered the first load of lumber and we began to

make the sills for the foundation. We already had pads and concrete blocks ready to begin. The first lumber unloaded was two by eight's made of oak.

Every time we tried to drive a nail we would bend it. We used many pounds of nails before we learned how to do it correctly. There was a kind black man who delivered the lumber. He said, "Let me show you how to nail these together to make the sills." He was a carpenter himself. He reached in his pocket, pulled out a little bar of soap, and said, "Now, you put a little soap on the nail and it will drive right through the hard oak." We tried it, and even Brother Lott learned a great truth that day and marveled at it along with the rest of us.

It was at that same time that Dr. Jimmy Hollingsworth built a new church in Springhill, Louisiana. He also used Mr. Lambert to finance his building. In our Springhill Association we had the two fastest growing churches. There was much similarity between Dr. Hollingsworth and me in our methods of preaching the gospel.

Many people were saved at that church, some of the hardest cases that Doyline has ever known. Many of the Burge family were saved. I clearly remember Billbo Burge and have always counted him a dear friend. He was a great guy and a very firm man. I buried him not long ago and reflected on many of these fond memories.

Billbo was the life of the party and a wonderful person. He would do anything he could to help at all times. He was a very plainspoken man. I will never forget, as a lost man, he was working on the church building. One day he hit his thumb with a hammer.

He threw the hammer down and cursed. I suddenly felt led to go to the other end of the building. Later he came to me and said, "Preacher, I'm sorry that I used that kind of language. I should not have done that." I said, "Billbo, I didn't mention it to you." He said, "It's a good thing you didn't, because I would have thrown my hammer at you at that moment."

I was then even more thankful that I had not rebuked him at that moment. There is a time for everything.

I remember when we were working on the baptistery together and many of the people were helping. We were all crowded around and finally, for the want of air, Billbo said, "All of you please get back. I might want to be baptized in this mess one day." That was the first indication that he was interested in his soul.

As time went on we had a great revival with fifty additions. One night, Brother Lott was preaching the revival and Billbo was attending. Billbo was anything but a hen-pecked husband, but we thought we would fool him that night. We asked all the henpecked husbands to come down and sit in the first few rows. He quickly came and sat in the front. Then we said, "The rest of you come on down, we know who you are. Winfred Palmer, we all know you are henpecked so come on down."

Billbo heard the gospel that night and from the second pew came and hugged me during the invitation. He said, "Preacher, I am turning it over to the Lord tonight." I said,

"Billbo, I am so happy to hear it. Let's kneel here and pray."
He said, "You misunderstood me. I have already turned it
over to the Lord." From that day forward he never missed a
lick in serving God. He was regular in attendance and always
so gracious to help. God bless his sweet memory.

There are many more fond memories of Trinity, our first
church. It was there that my brothers were baptized. I had
the sweet privilege of leading them to Christ. My dear mother, a Godly woman, was a Methodist. She was saved at the
age of fourteen. She didn't have the opportunity to grow in
grace like she would if she had attended regular services. She
neglected some spiritual things, but she was one of greatest
mothers that ever lived. She was, without a doubt, the hub
of our family.

I used to talk to my mother about doctrine because I
wanted to baptize her. She would say, "Jim, I will be with you
in Heaven." I said, "Yes, Mother, I know that. But I want
you to be scripturally baptized by immersion. I would love to
be your pastor."

There are some special rewards when you are a member of
a sound New Testament Church. The day came when my
dear mother walked the aisle for baptism along with my father.
My brother, George, came that day and surrendered to preach
the gospel. Everyone rejoiced and thanked God. There were
fourteen lined up in the front of our little church and
Heaven came down and thrilled our souls.

My mother became a Sunday School teacher. I had the
desire of my heart fulfilled by baptizing her and becoming her

pastor. This was the fruition of one of my dreams. She died in 1963 of pancreatitis. She often said that she hoped to live until my girls were old enough to court. She could not wait to see how I would react.

My two brothers are currently living in Sibley, La., and both attending Baptist Tabernacle there. George is married to Darlene Hollowell Tharpe. They have a nice family which consists of 5 children, 5 spouses, 9 grandchildren, and 11 great grandchildren.

Jack is married to Barbara Rainer Tharpe, and they also have a great family which includes 3 children, 3 spouses, and 6 grandchildren. It is a wonderful occasion when about 100 Tharpe's get together for a family reunion.

I lost my only sister when she was 8, but God has given me two sisters-in-law who are very special to me.

All along, God was training me in the School of Hard Knocks. I was preaching many revival meetings in surrounding churches and the devil took advantage of my absence. Members of the Pentecostal Church approached some of my young people. They were having a revival. This happened at the same time my vocal cords had been injured due to all the preaching and I had to have surgery.

I was ordered by the doctor not to speak a word for a certain amount of time to allow for healing following the surgery. He told me to carry a pad with me and write anything that needed to be said. Although I was told I was not to speak I knew I must talk to my young people. I had to protect them regardless of the possible injury to myself. So I did.

God blessed me greatly in the evangelistic field. Many souls were saved and lives changed as a result of the hard work. We had many laughs during the days of our young preachers, when I was away holding revivals.

I would be away almost all summer, and occasionally return to preach at Trinity. The other preachers would fill the pulpit and preach in my absence.

Finally, we had Tharpites, Holcombites, Petersonites, etc. and the church was divided. I came back to preach a sermon and touched on this subject. Many met at the altar and repented.

I remember what George preached the Sunday before I came back. He was scolding the people when he said, "We're down, but don't worry. Your God, Jimmy, will be back next Sunday." He was a hard hitter and we had a lot of laughs about his frustration over this.

We had several preachers to come out of Trinity. George Tharpe, David Peterson, Glenn Holcomb and Donald Hart were some of these. Many of these men made great marks for the Lord. I remember when David Peterson was saved. He was a Lutheran and had attended his church faithfully for many years. We were guards together at the Ordinance Plant when I invited him to church. Our church had tarpaper around the building before it was bricked. It was very different from the great cathedral type to which he was accustomed.

After the service that day, David came running down the aisle with his Bible opened. He said, "According to the Lutheran people I am saved, but according to the Bible I am lost." He came so fast we bumped heads and then fell to our knees where David accepted the Lord Jesus into his heart. I told him it did not matter what people said. As we all know, the only things that matter are what God says. David made a great preacher. He served on our staff many years and is currently pastoring a church on Lake Claiborne. He also serves on the faculty of Louisiana Baptist University. His wife, Verna, is a great preacher's wife and is one of our long time friends.

Shortly before receiving the call to pastor Baptist Tabernacle, I was still taking classes at Louisiana Baptist Seminary. One day Brother Clover stood up in the classroom and announced, "Dr. W.W. Miles, pastor of the great Fatherland Baptist Church of Nashville, Tennessee, has just contacted me. Pastor Miles is trying to locate Jimmy Tharpe to come and hold the first meeting in his new auditorium." At that time it was the largest among Missionary Baptists. Of course, it was a thrill, when Edith and I got to go to this huge church to preach their first revival. This was quite a surprise.

Folks had been trying to guess who would hold the first revival in the new church building. Some guessed Walter Lovelady and some guessed M.W. Melton. I never dreamed I would be the one chosen to hold this great revival.

It was there that God gave me the vision to return to Shreveport and build Baptist Tabernacle. I guess we built it as large as we did because of that vision. The revival meeting was a success. Many were saved, including a man who was studying to be a Catholic priest.

While pastoring Trinity Baptist Church, I took part in associational affairs. I helped in many churches in the local association. Brother Lott, our local and state missionary, began a new work in Shreveport, under the auspices of Central Baptist Church. He worked diligently constructing a two-story building and winning souls to add to the new church membership. I helped lay the cornerstone in the first building and also preached the first message.

Splits and Fights

On two occasions I stood for two hours before the local and state associations of the American Baptist Association trying to answer questions in order to work out some differences with some brethren.

I am a Baptist by conviction but an Independent Baptist by eviction. I care little about working in a unified group or organized religion. Some people are power hungry and shoot for the top. They do not care whom they step on along the way.

I dislike that attitude and would rather be completely independent. We are Baptists that go back to the "Sunny Shores Of Galilee" and will fellowship with any sound Baptist. Many of our critics later became friends and for that I am very thankful. Sometimes God will turn the bitterest enemy into the dearest friend.

Some of our best preacher friends have gone astray in the ministry. I weep untold tears when this occurs. I even spent time in the hospital once I was so distraught. I do not know anyone who hates to see the fall of a preacher more than I do. My prayers are always with them and I have an eagerness to help them in any way possible.

For two or three years I worked closely with the local and state associations. After an actual split in the group and some disagreement on policy, the Springhill Association withdrew fellowship from some of the member churches and pastors. A bitter misunderstanding caused the main group to exclude two of the preachers, Brother Foster Lott and Brother C.K. House. This caused a division in the seminary and the preachers chose sides according to their leaning.

Brother Lott was falsely accused of teaching heresy, which was in no way true. Brother House stood firmly with Brother Lott. At a mission rally in Bossier City, Louisiana, Brother Clover stood and openly came out against the two men. After this, Brother Lott and Brother House joined Hope Baptist Church in Heflin, Louisiana.

I believe I owe a great deal to Missionary Baptists. Because of them I was taught true doctrine. I have often said they were doctrinally sound but dispositionally wrong.

Sadly, there is still animosity between some who took different sides. At a funeral at Old Sarepta Baptist Church, Brother Clover and I found ourselves working together. We were able to work out our differences. He told me, "I am proud of your accomplishments. You were one of the most promising students we had in the Seminary." It was not too long after this that he died. I visited with Mrs. Clover and she gave me many of his books that I cherish to this day.

When the split came in the Springhill Association I did not take the Associational stand. I chose to follow my true convictions and stand for what I believed in. When I stood against the exclusion of Foster Lott and C.K. House, the bottom seemed to fall out for me. A meeting of the ABA leaders was called immediately at Calvary Baptist Church in Minden, Louisiana.

I tried to stave off a split by saying; "This matter you are dealing with is between two sovereign churches, namely Hope Baptist Church in Heflin, Louisiana, and Calvary Baptist Church in Minden, Louisiana." But the entire ABA group met and excluded Foster Lott and C.K. House. Anyone who associated with them was out of fellowship with the state and local association as well. Naturally, I loved these two men dearly. They had been my spiritual leaders and helped make me what I am today. But that was not really the issue.

I stood with them because I felt they were excluded without a cause. Hope Church as well as other churches out of the association took them in. I remember Mr. Lawrence Brunson saying to his church, "We feel these men were unjustly excluded and we have a right to receive them." It was there that I took my stand. We had only six churches to fellowship with. Many preachers began to fight without a cause.

We were later excommunicated from the local and state association and even from Boggs Springs Youth Encampment where we had taken our young people for many years. Out of that experience came the vision to build our own Youth Encampment.

I was even accused of "pulpit affiliation" because I had some great preachers to preach in my pulpit who were not Missionary Baptists.

The call comes

I dearly loved Trinity Baptist Church, so when Tabernacle Baptist called me to be their pastor, it was compelling. I prayed about it and decided this was where God wanted me to be. Resigning Trinity was a very sad time for me. Even little children hugged me and wept saying, "Brother Tharpe, you are not going to leave us are you?" It was so emotionally overwhelming that I was not able to finish what I had planned to say.

My deacons had to take me home where I continued to weep all night. The pain of standing before my congregation and saying good-bye was something I didn't want to experience again. I knew at that moment I never wanted to resign another church.

CHAPTER 4

THE TABERNACLE YEARS

I have worked with Baptist Tabernacle since it's beginning. When the church was ready to call a pastor, I was chosen. It was a much larger field with opportunities unlimited to work for the Lord.

On that first Sunday there, God taught us a great lesson in faith.

Our Debbye was just a little baby. It was time for her to eat and we had run out of milk. We had misfigured our pennies when we moved and lacked one dime having enough to buy a quart of milk. Of course, to ask someone for a dime would be embarrassing. I walked over to open the doors of the little white frame building for Sunday services. As I walked along, with my head down, I noticed one shiny dime lying on the windswept churchyard. I picked it up, took it home, and Edith and I shed tears of joy. I quickly went across Hollywood Avenue to the Fil-A-Bil and got a quart of milk for the baby. I can assure you that on that day, and every day since, God has supplied all our needs according to His riches in glory. That little dime meant the world to me.

It was very different when I moved my family to Shreveport. My wife and four children were accustomed to the country church at Doyline and when we came to the city there was a bit of a stiff feeling. We didn't want our children to go into nice homes and cause any problems. There were times when we felt the city church could not compare to the country church. At first, Edith and the kids wanted to go back home, but soon grew to love the people and knew they were in the right place.

The first Sunday at Tabernacle, we went home with Mary and L. G. Morris for lunch. Brother Lott had spoken to us about going into the homes with all the children and to be very careful. We had worried about our children's behavior, but we never thought that Kathy would be the one to cause a problem. She was the oldest and so quiet and timid.

She was lying on the floor right beside an upholstered stool. Somehow, she put a big upholstery tack in her mouth and accidentally swallowed it. We called the doctor and he said, "Don't worry about it. God fixed it where the tack usually turns point up and goes through with no problem. However, if she has bleeding, get her here immediately." Edith was still afraid so we took her for an x-ray. Thank

God, it was head down, point up as the doctor had said it would be. The other children behaved nicely and that eased some of our fears.

The church had already built one white two-story building where we had many good services. When we came to Shreveport, the salary agreed upon was $75 per week. I had Edith, four babies, and an old car. We had rented a house from Don Turner.

The house was on Hollywood Avenue next door to where the church is now. Soon Don and his wife came into the church and worked faithfully with us for a long time. I began to preach with a vision of building Baptist Tabernacle and growing in numbers.

We got into a bond program to finance the new auditorium. Brother Lott didn't think we could sell the five percent debenture bonds. We ended up in the office of Mrs. Nellie Kilpatrick, owner of an insurance company. She often purchased bonds and asked us how many we had. I told her $50,000 and she agreed to take them all. She made me a happy man that day. When I returned to the church I called the men and we celebrated by going together to the bank and making that BIG deposit. We were now underway with the first big vision and the great work of the Tabernacle began.

I preached hard and continued with the vision of building Baptist Tabernacle. We were selling bonds and growing in numbers. God began to bless. I know our small number of people must have been scared to death to take on that big indebtedness, but they followed my leadership.

When I was chided for leading them into such a big building, someone asked where we would be if they had balked. The answer was, "We would still be in that white two-story building." For two years and three months we worked on that auditorium. Some of the men put in so many hours for the Lord, I thought there might be some divorces. We had some very irritated wives because they were away from home for so many hours.

We had such a faithful group of people and God tremendously blessed us. Baptist Tabernacle auditorium seated twelve hundred people and later provided the place for the commencement services for the schools. We have always felt that the more ministries a church can have the better off that church will be. It adds strength in many areas.

I remember one preacher came and stood watching as we worked on the new auditorium. He looked all around at the massive structure and said, "This is a monstrosity." The definition of monstrosity is oversized and out of proportion. I believe he was right, however, many have been saved at Baptist Tabernacle. Many have gone on to preach the gospel and close to one hundred churches have been established as a result. This leads me to believe that we need more monstrosities in the world. And might I add, that that "monstrosity" was filled to capacity, standing room only, on many occasions.

The day finally came for the dedication of the beautiful building. We had many of our bond holders there and other dignitaries including Mayor Clyde Fant. The Mayor was a remarkable person and instrumental in helping us in so many ways. I introduced him by saying, "I am so glad my people get to meet you, Mayor, we have heard a lot about you." He replied, "They can't prove it all." We all laughed together. He was such a great Mayor and did a lot for the church to make the dedication day possible.

According to the utility provider we were not going to be able to have electricity for the grand opening of the sanctuary. I called Mayor Fant. There happened to be two trucks from the electric company going down Hollywood Avenue right at that moment. They were dispatched after a call from the Mayor and we had electricity in ten minutes. We were very thankful.

Foster Lott preached the dedication message and did a wonderful job. He told a story of a boy who had a little red wagon. The boy asked all the little girls for a kiss. He was refused many times. Finally, a little girl said yes. The boy said, "Now what do I do?" Brother Lott ended his sermon by raising his hands in the air and saying, "You have done a great job getting this far, now what will you do?" I have often said to myself, "where do we go from here?" We definitely went farther than we had ever dreamed and we owe it all to God.

The next few years were wonderful for the church and my family. They both grew and grew. We had many additions to the church and two more to my family, Roger and Brenda, giving us six to keep up with.

One Sunday morning I had gone to church early and left Edith to later bring the five children we had at that time. She got all of them ready and put them on the couch to wait for her while she got dressed. Don Turner had moved the house we lived in further back on his property and had done a lot of dirt work in the process. It had rained for several days. Edith noticed that the children were very quiet so she went to see about them. She was going to take them to the church in the car, but as you can guess, the Tharpe family missed church that day. Every one of them had mud from their head to their toes. Their mother was still in tears when I got home because it was red mud and their clothes were ruined.

Days went by and my mind was filled with new visions as to how we could reach people for the Lord. The following is a list of some of the ministries that we developed:

Baptist Christian College

Baptist Christian Academy

Baptist Christian University

Louisiana Baptist University

Baptist Christian Youth Encampment

Baptist Christian Boys Home

Baptist Christian Publications

Tabernacle Radio and Television Ministry

Tabernacle Counseling Center

Tabernacle Deaf Ministry

Tabernacle Recreational Recovery Center

Joy Club

Museum

Mission Churches

Baptist Tabernacle has sent out seventy-five churches and many of these are still doing business for the Lord. One of the most recent was a work between Sibley and Minden near my hometown. This is the second independent Baptist church we built in Sibley. A building was built in nine months and a mission established. I would drive there and preach at 9:00 am and hurry back to Baptist Tabernacle to preach the morning services on Sunday. After two years and three months we built a beautiful building and an educational building completely debt free. Dr. Morris Robe was called as the first pastor of that church and still pastor's there today. This is probably one of the most outstanding works I can think of.

Many of these churches were built in our city, such as Shreveport Baptist Temple where Dr. Howard Hall is pastor, Berean Baptist where Dr. Randy Johnson is pastor, and Northside Baptist, which later changed its name to Indian Hills, that was pastored for years by Dr. Corbitt Mask. You can go any direction and see churches that were planted by Baptist Tabernacle. Waskom Baptist Temple is right across the Texas line, and there is Baptist Tabernacle, in Longview, Texas, where many of our graduates have pastored.

The 75th mission church we have sent out is in Benton, Louisiana, where Brother Jimmy Hollingsworth is now working. He thought he was ready to retire and teach in the Louisiana School of Prophets, but he came to the conclusion he wanted to get back to pastoring. God bless him as he starts this mission.

Friends of the church

Louie Grafton

Louie Grafton along with his wife, Betty, have been pillars

of strength in Baptist Tabernacle for nearly the same length of time that I have. Mrs. Grafton has worked in many areas....secretary to the pastor, teacher in the Academy, and wherever her help was needed. She is now teaching in Shreveport Christian Academy. Long ago, when teaching at the high school level, before she came to class one morning, two of the boys got in a pretty bad fight in the classroom. By then, they were down in the floor when Mrs. Grafton walked in and in her usual way, went to where they were. Without a word, she got hold of the hair at the hairline of the one on top. He was willing to give up the fight as she pulled him up by the hair.

Mr. Grafton, better known as Papa Louie, is now 82 years old and still working at the church. He has been a kind, wonderful deacon and maintenance supervisor for all these years. He sees to the comfort of our people. He has always been so easy to work with, so caring for his pastor, church, and the mechanics of its operations. Mr. Grafton worked a full-time job at the Shreveport Times, but was at the church and school very early in the mornings to see that the heat or air was on and everything was ready to start the day. He was back again in the afternoons to close everything down for the night. He gave a feeling of security for us all. Once we had two fires in one week. He helped to clean up and repair all the damage. I cannot express the gratitude we all feel for one so dear. They were members at Trinity before they came to us. Many years ago, Brother Louie was the only deacon who did not walk out of a meeting. I thought they all had gone. I folded my face in my hands and began to cry. I looked up and there stood Brother Louie, the only one who stood with me in that particular time. This was an exception to the rule and of course we worked it out.

Clayton Weaver

If I had to try to state the many ways Clayton and Linda Weaver have been a blessing to me, my wife, and my children, I wouldn't know how to start. Brother Clayton has been on our staff as a deacon and spiritual leader for 42 years. Linda has worked in every part of the church and school, from taking care of flowers for the sanctuary to church secretary. Linda is one of the kindest, gentlest, compassionate Christian women in the church. They are the kind of team that every pastor would love to have. Many times people have said, "I really need a 'Clayton' in my church. He has been financial director for the church and schools for many years and has really taken care of that job well. When there is a death in our membership, he takes care of the necessities, such as food, flowers, etc. In every area of the church, they have so much knowledge of records that everyone calls them when there is a question. He also held a full-time job and worked tirelessly after hours for the church and school.

In 1998, when construction on the new church was in progress, I was hospitalized with a severe stroke. No one knew at that time how I was going to be able to function or even if I was going to live. We had a construction crew out of Tennessee who were working on the building. Because of the stroke I was unable to help in any way.

The man who accepted the responsibility and saw that the work continued was Clayton Weaver. Clayton took full responsibility as Director and carried the building on to completion. I will be eternally grateful for his outstanding role of leadership during the time when I was totally disabled. Words cannot express how grateful Edith and I are for the love and care that the Weavers have shown us.

Bill Kincaid

Bill came to us from Odessa, Texas as a student of Baptist Christian College. He earned his bachelor's degree as he did volunteer work at the church. Bill is a very loyal, dedicated and sincere Christian who has worked diligently on the staff for 34 years. He has served faithfully in every capacity of the work, even once operating a print shop.

Bill showed willingness and patience and has always done more than his job required. He teaches the Auditorium Bible Class in Sunday School, administers the visitation program, Men's Brotherhood, and many other activities.

Bill's wife, Linda, is an example of what a Christian wife should be. She was one of the first students who came to Baptist Christian and met and married Bill in our church. She also teaches Sunday School, teaches school at Sunset Acres Elementary, and keeps up a card ministry for the whole church. If it's your birthday, anniversary, or you are sick, you can expect a card from her and Brother Bill. They are an integral part of Baptist Tabernacle as they pray daily for the church membership.

James Camp

Brother James has 23 years of service at Baptist Tabernacle as our music and choir director. He is an excellent music man and the best platform man I have ever known. I cannot say enough about Brother Camp, or give him the credit that he deserves for being such a blessing to our church. He is a tireless worker in so many other areas too. His wife, Sue, worked side by side with my wife at the Baptist Christian Book Store and as bookkeeper in the financial office.

Don Edwards

Don has been a member of Baptist Tabernacle since he was a teenager. He along with, his mother, and sister were some of the first members we had when we moved to Shreveport. Don is an extremely gifted and talented individual. He discovered his talent for art after he was older and has now become a nationally renowned wildlife artist. He is also a photographer and has traveled to the Holy Land, Africa, the Rockies (and many other locations) to take pictures of wildlife, landscapes, etc.

His talents continue through his world class paintings, based on pictures taken on location. He is a loyal, dedicated Christian man who loves his church. Don's wife, Sandy, is musically talented, and is the church pianist. She works hard and gives her time for church services, choir practices, and solo accompaniment. She is very important to the church where she is rarely absent. Sandy was also the school and church secretary for a period of time.

Nelda Cooper

Nelda and Loyd Cooper moved to Shreveport from Arkansas years ago when Nelda's brother, Glen, came to enroll in the college. Her parents, Mr. and Mrs. Frank Ridings, also moved here and worked in the church and school. Frank was a deacon in the church.

The Coopers had young children in the Academy so Nelda started working in the school. From that day to this, she has served the schools and church in every possible area and is willing to do anything, anytime. She will take on jobs that nobody else will do and doesn't mind it a bit as long as it's for the Lord. Loyd helped me transcribe the tapes for this book and put the initial draft on the computer.

We have so many wonderful Christians who have this same attitude toward doing their part to promote the ministries of the church. They have all been a real blessing in my life.

I won't try to name everyone who has served with us for fear of inadvertently leaving someone out. I appreciate all those who have served with me in the Lord's work and wish I had space to name them. Trust me when I say that I value and love everyone that has worked with me, and that I know there is a great reward for all who have been so faithful in His ministry.

Ministries of the church

Deaf Ministry

One of my ministries was with Don Cabbage, son-in-law of Bill Rice, who led a deaf ministry and had a very successful revival in our church years ago. We have had a deaf ministry since that day.

Brother Don told us about the earlier years of his marriage. His wife was deaf and when they got into a fuss, she would sign to him exactly how she felt, and then quickly turn her head so as not to see his reply.

Brother Bill Kincaid and his dear wife Linda head that ministry today. They still use it for the glory of God.

Baptist Christian College

I remember shortly after we arrived in Shreveport we began praying about a college. My heart was thrilled when we began Baptist Christian College in 1961.

Baptist Christian Academy

In 1964, Baptist Christian Academy was started, grades one through twelve. The academy at one time had a total of six hundred thirty-nine students.

Baptist Christian University

In 1973, Baptist Christian University was started. Not much later, Baptist Christian Youth Encampment began on eleven acres of land. One day we baptized fifty-two at Dorcheat where the Youth Encampment was located. Later, we had a Baptist Christian Radio Program and Television ministry. This also proved to be profitable.

Other Ministries

We had Baptist Christian Publications Ministry under the direction of Brother Bill Kincaid, who has done a wonderful job through the years in every phase of work imaginable. We also established a ministry to help folks through difficult times, the Baptist Christian Counseling Center, under the direction of Dr. David Peterson. He had the center on the campus of Baptist Tabernacle and Baptist Christian College.

Youth Ministries

One of the sweetest memories was the Youth Ministry of Baptist Tabernacle. We had eleven buildings on eighteen acres of land on beautiful Lake Dorcheat. We enjoyed summer camps, Bible Conferences, and many other great times in the Lord. We had fifty people saved and baptized in one meeting in the early years of Baptist Christian Youth Encampment. Brother Jim Murphy was administrator of the church and Youth Director. He built the youth ministry to its highest level when he was here.

Later, the youth encampment became Baptist Christian Boys Home. At one time we had thirty-six boys living there and serving God. Hundreds of people have been saved through that ministry, for which we are grateful. Many changes were made and homes rearranged through that ministry.

Joy Club

The Joy Club was instituted as a program for our older people. Mrs. Maxine Schepp, one of our first church members, has been involved in this ministry for many years. There are monthly meetings where we have trips, speakers, fellowship, and great food.

The letters JOY stands for Just Old Youth and that is exactly what we are. I have been a member of the club for some time now. They are some of our very best church members and are very dedicated to Baptist Tabernacle.

Museum

Don Edwards and I have paid the cost of building a museum as a gift to Baptist Tabernacle. It is a wildlife museum which houses many mounts including my bear, an alligator, deer, snakes, and many other animals.

School Of The Prophets of Louisiana

Just recently, Dr. Jimmy Hollingsworth, who graduated with a doctors degree from Baptist Christian University, prayed with me about starting a new preachers school to train only preachers. Even this year, two missions have been sent out and God has given us preachers for them. This is from our church and has worked successfully. We are excited about this because it has enabled us together to put in a total of 100 years knowledge and experience for the young preachers to learn from.

Publications

For many years, I was editor of *The Soulwinner*, a paper that had a circulation of 3,000 and was sent out monthly. *The Eagles View* is now the official paper of the University.

I wrote several booklets including, *Bread from Tabernacle's Table*, *Great Monuments of the New Testament Church*, *Comfort*, and *How to Turn Bitterness to Sweetness*. God really has used the *Comfort* book in ministering to grieving families. When someone loses a family member, I send the *Comfort* book.

CHAPTER 5

FRIENDS OF THE MINISTRY

Whitfield Jack

A great man, who was a friend to our work, was Whitfield Jack. He and his brother were noted attorneys in our city. I remember when we needed an attorney to represent us at the Securities and Exchange Commission in Washington, DC. It was on December 23 that I called Mr. Jack and asked if he knew of an attorney, at this late hour, that I could get to go to Washington with me. This meeting with the SEC was due to the handling and sale of bonds to build our buildings. They were investigating our sale of bonds.

This meeting with the Securities and Exchange

Commission had come about because we had gotten behind in payments of the bond coupons. I had been previously called to Fort Worth by the SEC to answer some questions.

I had served as my own attorney on five or six different occasions because we didn't have the money to hire anyone. The chief administrator had told me that we had to go into bankruptcy within two weeks. He had yelled at me and I yelled back telling him that he would not speak to me in that tone of voice. It was then that I decided to call Mr. Jack and get someone to go with me to Washington.

He said, "Reverend, I don't know anyone you could get, this near to Christmas. Let me call you back, though." And in ten minutes, he did. His words to me were, "I don't understand this, I thought I couldn't go. I have company coming in, but somehow, I must go with you. You get the tickets, and be on time. I am going to Washington with you myself."

I didn't have any money so I checked with Dr. Bill McCormack, who was representing all of America for the Washington, D.C Bureau of Alcohol and Tobacco. He had a suite next to the Capitol and graciously let us use it. Mr. Jack met me, as he had said he would. Before we were airborne, he put his hand on my knee, and said, "Reverend, I know you don't have any money. My services cost $40 an hour, and you couldn't afford them anyway. This won't cost you a dime."

He took a little yellow sheet of paper and began to ask me questions. I had not handled the money, never have, and I did not know the answer to many questions. It was hard to be your own attorney, when you didn't know how to be.

I answered as best I could, and sometimes he would even get a little upset because I didn't know. This would make me feel bad about it. Sometimes Mr. Jack would use a little "slang" word, and then say, "Excuse me, Reverend. You know I am an Episcopalian." I would answer, "That's all right, sir."

He worked all the way to Washington, and when we got to the suite, I went over and raised some windows. He said, "Don't do that. You're in DC now. Leave the windows down." I obeyed him, and shortly thereafter a policeman came and asked if we called for him. We responded that we did not. The policeman said, "Well somebody did. Last week there were forty something windows broken on automobiles in front of this building." When the officer left, I said, "I see what you mean now, Mr. Jack."

We then went to the chief administrator's office of the SEC in Washington. The man was looking out the window, paying little attention to Mr. Jack. Finally, Mr. Jack said, "Say, look here at me young man. You're talking to a top-flight attorney. You'll either look at me now, or you'll look at me in court. I am a bondholder, and I represent him as well. Now which one do you want?"

That got his attention. Mr. Jack went on to tell him that I had built a good work in our city, using a little off color word. I almost said, 'Amen.' Then he asked me to excuse them and to step outside. I knew what he was trying to do then. He was trying to patch some things up with the government man, and he did. He was such a gracious man.

After the trip to Washington, I went back to the SEC in

Fort Worth. The administrator there said to me, "Well, I see you went over my head." I said, "Yes, I did and I'll do it again, because I knew you couldn't force me into bankruptcy."

The outcome of all this was that we were cleared of any wrongdoing. The last thing the administrator said to me as we left was, "Don't go back and put anything else on the drawing board." My response to him was, "As a matter of fact, we already have a gymnasium on the drawing board." He just raised his hands and jokingly told me, "Just get out of here."

Some years later, I saw Mr. Jack, and after showing him my appreciation, because of present illness he failed to remember the incident. I was sorry of that because he had meant so much to me.

Lash LaRue

The Church has reached many wonderful people including the movie star, Lash LaRue, who was King of the Bullwhip. I was visiting with Dr. Don Chelette in Alexandria, Louisiana. On this occasion, we were knocking doors and trying to win souls to Christ. We visited in the home of a young lady who had been attending Brother Don's church. We had no idea she was the daughter of Lash LaRue.

When we walked inside, a man was sitting there wearing dark glasses. I said, "Don't I know who you are?" He said, "No, I don't think you do." Later, in the visit, I asked again and the friend that was with him said, "Yes, he is modest and won't tell you but I will. He is Lash LaRue, the movie star."

I said, "Lash LaRue! I have spent my last quarter many

times to see you in a double feature at the Joy Theater in Minden, Louisiana. I loved to watch you round up the criminals with your whip. I cannot believe I am looking into the face of Lash Larue."

Brother Don and I talked to him and we shared many things together. I then asked the question of all questions. "Lash, I want to ask you the most important question you will ever hear. Do you know Jesus as your Savior?" He said, "I am glad you asked me that. I am happy to tell you that I am saved."

He then went on to testify for us, "I was down in Las Vegas attending the cash register for a friend. A group of Christians were there holding a meeting. I stood in the doorway and listened at the close of the meeting. The speaker asked, "Is there any one here who does not know Christ who would like to be saved?"

"I lifted my hand and a personal worker came to me. I was led into a room and directed to Jesus Christ. I know I was saved that day, but later I became disillusioned with Hollywood. To tell you the truth, I am looking for a place to die."

I said, "Lash, you are still a young man and you should be looking for a place to live." I challenged him to take his Bible and bullwhip and lead boys and girls to Christ. He said, "The bullwhip is in my car. I don't take it out much, but I do practice with it from time to time."

I urged him to pray about it and he said he would. We spoke over the phone several times after that day. I challenged him to come to Baptist Tabernacle and let me set up a "Lash

LaRue Day." I wanted him to come and give his testimony. He accepted my invitation and said he would like to follow the Lord in baptism on that day.

He came, and we had a wonderful service in our gymnasium. There were thirty-seven people saved in the gym that day. He cut paper from the mouth of Debbye, my daughter, with his whip. We all rejoiced over Lash Larue and his testimony. I introduced Lash to others and several churches invited him to give his testimony and he accepted.

Lash still visits me from time to time. The last time he was here, I put his Hollywood guns on and took a picture with him. I have not seen him in a while now, but will always count him a dear friend.

Billy Francis

During my childhood years, a young boy came to live with my family. His name was Billy Francis and he loved our entire family, and my mother treated him like one of her sons. I remember Billy especially loved mom's breakfast of hot buttered biscuits and hot chocolate. Billy had a difficult childhood and needed a family to take care of him.

Billy was one of us and when he reached the eighth grade he began to work on automobiles. He had a great inventor's mind that later proved to be very successful for him. He developed the Major Mud and Chemical Company, and he also had seven profitable inventions. He even invented a product for helping with the mud used in drilling.

Billy became a multimillionaire, but he never forgot the

Tharpe family. Many times he would have us come to his thousand acre duck camp and the whole family enjoyed sweet fellowship. Later in life he donated a lot of money to Baptist Christian Boys Home. He seemed to love the boys and supported many of them. His total contributions were over $300,000.

I remember when Billy was sending $10,000 per month to our boys. While Billy was there visiting one day, Little Tommy, one of nineteen boys in the home, came out and asked for a thousand dollars for each of the boys.

Billy asked what Tommy thought he would do with the money. Tommy pointed to the director and said, "I would give it to him." Billy did not say anything at the time, but later said, "Tell the little fellow that came to me that his wishes are granted." Billy went back home and sent us a check for $19,000.

When little Tommy first asked the question I looked at him as if to say, "Get lost boy, we are trying to do business for the Lord." Then Mr. Jones, the director, told him to go back into the house. After Billy told us he would give us the money, I wanted to go find Tommy and wear him out for not asking for $100,000.

Billy later was stricken with cancer and in a few months went home to be with the Lord. I had spoken with Billy many times about his soul but never had the full assurance that he had been saved.

One night, he asked me to sit up with him all night at the duck camp while others slept. We talked until daybreak. Still, I was unsettled on the issue of his salvation and because of his increasing illness I was compelled to talk to him again.

He was in the hospital in Lafayette, Louisiana. I asked my two brothers to take his wife for coffee and give me a few minutes alone with him. I started by saying, "Billy, I have never had the assurance you were really saved and I have to ask you again about your soul."

He sat up in his bed and said, "Jim, I have been thinking about this more than you would know, especially in the last couple of weeks." I said, "Bill, I would like for you to receive Christ as your personal Savior." "Let's do it now!" He replied. After I showed him the plan of redemption, Billy was gloriously saved. We both wept convulsively.

Larry Norrell

One of the good times in my ministry was meeting Larry Norrell. He came to ask me for a job at Baptist Christian Academy. I liked Larry the first time I met him, but told him I could not hire him because he was a Freewill Baptist and believed in falling from grace.

Larry was very kind hearted and we had a long talk about doctrine. He had been exposed to our faith in the concept of "once saved, always saved" when he attended a meeting with Dr. Jack Hyles and Dr. John R. Rice. He told me about that meeting.

He later was interested in joining our church and said he was going to pray about it. I looked up one Sunday night and his entire congregation was coming into our church. I suddenly changed my sermon to "Once Saved, Always Saved."

After the service they all walked the aisle for baptism. I asked the church to give Larry the authority to baptize his entire congregation who joined our church that night. The church agreed and we had a grand baptism. Larry baptized until he completely gave out. There was only one of his men that did not accept the doctrine that night, but later he did. Larry is still a dear friend of mine.

Larry has had a colorful history in the ministry. He was called as an assistant to Dr. Homer Ritchie at First Baptist Church in Fort Worth, Texas. Later he became pastor at Central Baptist Church in Tyler, Texas.

When he was in Tyler, there was a time when he got a little too big for his britches, playing practical jokes on me and others. On one occasion, when he knew we were having financial difficulty at the college, he called me one evening.

He told me to come to Tyler, a two-hour drive, to pick up a big check he had for the college. I was sick, but I went anyway. James Camp agreed to make the drive with me, and we headed to Texas.

When we arrived, Larry pulled out a check for $150,000. Visions of what could be done with that check were flying through my head. I was so thankful for this gift. Then he took the check, and tore it up as I stood there watching.

It felt as if he tore my heart up along with the check. Then he took out another blank check and handed it to me. I tried not to let him see how disappointed I really was. I told him, "Larry, I will get you back for this if it's the last thing I do."

I let several weeks pass, and then decided to make my promise good to Larry. It took a lot of planning and several phone calls, but soon my plan was in motion.

I had two preachers call Larry to preach a joint meeting in Knoxville. Larry was excited, and ready to go share his knowledge with the congregation. When he arrived at the airport, the preacher picked him up and took him to a restaurant where we were all waiting.

Larry entered the restaurant to see Edith and me sitting with the church staff. He was surprised to see us there and said. "What in the world are you doing here?" I said, "We were passing through on our way to a revival and stopped by to have lunch and a little fellowship with you."

We all ordered steak and dessert. I had earlier arranged for Dr. Johnny Ramsey and Dr. John Rawlings to call and tie him up on the phone so we could eat his steak and dessert while he was on the phone. After the meal, I told him the sad news, there were no services planned here and he was not needed.

Also unknown to Larry, I had a credit card belonging to him and presented it to pay for the meal. When the card was returned after the meal was paid for, people began to pass it around. When it got to Larry he said, "This is my card! How did you get my card?"

Not only had he missed eating his dinner, he had paid for everyone else's. I told him that the card had been in my possession for some time. I said, "I enjoyed paying for the meal, and all the items we bought at the store, including my nice new briefcase. I would like to thank you, Larry, for your kind hospitality." I left him there bewildered and I headed on to New Castle, Delaware where I was scheduled to preach.

He had been warned not to fool with me. People told him that he would end up on the short end of the stick. When I returned to Shreveport I wrote him a letter myself, pretending to be Don Chelette.

I told Larry it is better not to fool with Brother Jimmy. I told him that I would call off the dogs if I were you. Larry got to worrying, and made a special trip to Shreveport. He put his hand out and said, "Dr. Tharpe, I would like to call a truce. If you will not fool with me I promise not to fool with you. We will call it even." I agreed with him. He never knew I was the one that wrote that letter, but he was forever cured of practical joking with me.

Roy Westmoreland

Dr. Roy Westmoreland and his wife, Laverne, long time friends, were hard workers and great soul winners. Two of their sons, Ron and Tim, were students of Baptist Christian College where Ron graduated.

Brother Westmoreland pastored Bethel Baptist Church in Memphis, Tennessee, for many years and was a great preacher. Since he died, Ron became pastor and has built a beautiful new church plant on large acreage. The church membership is growing fast.

Julian Pope

Julian Pope, and his wife, Evelyn, were members of

Baptist Tabernacle for five years and did a great work in Missions. While he was here he organized the Beams Ministry (Bible Education and Missionary Service). The purpose of this ministry was to provide scriptures for missionaries overseas.

Prior to that, he had organized many churches such as Calvary Baptist in Minden, Louisiana, and Central Baptist in Shreveport, our mother church. His son, Johnny, was a student at Baptist Christian and at one point it looked as if he would be my son-in-law. Johnny followed in his father's footsteps and went on to do great things for the Lord.

G.S. Lorne

Brother G.S. Lorne, the Apostle Paul of India, ministered to thousands and established many churches. His daughter, Queenie, lived with us for a time while she was enrolled in Baptist Christian College (BCC). She was a delight to watch as she adapted to our customs.

Queenie had never seen a TV, pantyhose, shampoo, toothpaste, deodorant, and many other things we take for granted. Soon, she was becoming so Americanized in her dress and hairstyle, that when Brother Lorne came to visit he took her back home to India. When she first came she was wearing typical Indian dresses and had long beautiful hair.

Brother Lorne didn't want her to get away from Indian customs because she was to be married to Matthew Henry, a young Indian preacher. We certainly missed her when she went home.

Orpha Rodriguez

Another foreign student lived in our home for some time. Her name was Orpha Rodriguez, daughter of Brother Isiah Rodriguez, whom we referred to as the "Apostle Paul to Mexico." She was more used to American ways than Queenie, but she was always homesick for Mexico and couldn't wait to get back.

During this same time span, Enrique Garay, a Mexican singer, stayed in our home. It has been said that the Tharpe's housed and fed more people that anybody else ever had. Our home has always had an open door policy.

A.J. Wall

Brother A.J. Wall and his wife, Ruth, also lived with us for a short time before organizing the Gilmer Road Baptist Church in Longview, Texas. They are great long time friends of Edith and me.

The church is now named Baptist Tabernacle and is one of our mission churches. Brother Wall has since gone to live with the Lord, and Ruth lives in Oklahoma. He left us with many precious memories.

Renee Freret

Renee Freret of Gulfport, Mississippi, came by my office one day for a visit. After having an unhappy relationship with a church in Arkansas, he was ready for a change and was seeking the Lord's will for his life. I offered him a job in the bus ministry, which he gladly accepted. He moved Frieda and the children to Shreveport and went to work.

Renee did an excellent job on the buses and was able to earn his degree while he was here. Later, he moved to Gulfport, Mississippi, where he built a great church and pastored for years. When he retired from the ministry, he took over Dr. Julian Pope's BEAMS ministry. Dr. Johnny Pope had prayed to keep this ministry going. Brother Freret has done a magnificent job for the Lord and the ministry was expanded to include "conducting mission conferences in churches, promoting and raising funds for missions, sending scriptures, Bible courses and other literature to missionaries, and going overseas for evangelistic campaigns and Bible seminars."

John Rawlings

Dr. John Rawlings, one of my heroes, has meant so much to me through the years. Several years ago in Florida, he brought me up on stage and introduced me to the Baptist Bible Fellowship. I spoke to them briefly and then Dr. Rawlings jokingly told me to get my tail off the platform. Everyone had a good laugh. This was the meeting where the body approved Baptist Christian and Liberty Baptist as fellowship schools. I was privileged to sit next to Jerry Falwell as this action took place.

Later, Dr. Rawlings was instrumental in sending Baptist Christian College more than $100,000 in a short period of time. I had always preached that God was able to supply our every need and we were grateful to Dr. Rawlings for helping us. I've learned so much from his wisdom.

I've called Dr. Rawlings many times and asked him, "What do I do now?" He came to preach and brought his lovely wife on one of my anniversaries and endeared himself to our people. He has sent the college much money to help and support us when we had nowhere to turn. Thank God for our wonderful older preachers.

Don Chelette

Dr. Don Chelette, who rededicated his life under my ministry, followed me one summer in revival meetings. At the close of the summer he surrendered to preach the gospel. He has been an outstanding man of God since that day.

He first built and then pastored Hope Baptist Church for thirty-one years. We have traveled many thousands of miles together. He and his dear wife, Louise, are two of the best friends Edith and I have ever had. We love them dearly.

Morris Robe

Dr. Morris Robe became a member of Baptist Tabernacle shortly after I came to Shreveport. It was Dr. Robe who attended the Minden Seminary with me and also graduated from Baptist Christian College. He and his wife, Elaine, worked on our staff for twenty-eight years.

Dr. Robe and his family have always been a tremendous blessing to me. He stuck with me through the hard years and his is a friendship I will always value. Dr. Robe headed our Bible Department for many years, and was Associate Pastor of Baptist Tabernacle. He has been successful in the ministry and is now pastor of Baptist Tabernacle, our Mission Church in Sibley, Louisiana.

Lee Roberson

Dr. Lee Roberson has always been my hero. He stands head and shoulders above most preachers I've ever known. I told him this one-day and he appreciated it very much. It was his vision that motivated me to build and grow. He has been in our church many times.

An Honorary Doctorate from Tennessee Temple College, a Doctor of Laws is one of the most precious I have ever received. One of my proudest days was when Dr. Lee conferred this degree on me. Another degree that I will always cherish is from Dr. Tom Malone at Midwestern Seminary.

R.G. Lee

Once, at Rolling Hills Baptist Church, I was scheduled to preach right before R.G. Lee. That night he was preaching his famous sermon, "Payday, Someday." I was to be the first speaker.

Someone asked me if I was afraid to preach in front of Dr. Lee. "Doesn't his presence bother you?" they asked. I made the statement that as much as I loved Dr. Lee, I had been preaching in the presence of the Lord Jesus Christ for many years and would surely not mind preaching in the presence of Dr. Lee.

When I got in the pulpit, I started out as if I was going to do his work, "I bring you Naboth, and I am preaching tonight on Payday Someday." Dr. Lee was sitting on the front pew. He clapped his hands and stomped his feet because he thought it was so funny.

Johnny Ramsey

Dr. Johnny Ramsey introduced me to a large number of Independent Baptist preachers. I preached at Rolling Hills Baptist Church with great men of God such as Dr. R.G. Lee, Dr. Tom Malone, Dr. Monroe Parker, Dr. Beachum Vick, Dr. J. Harold Smith, Dr. Lee Roberson, Dr. John R. Rice, Dr. Jack Hyles, Dr. Harold Sightler, Dr. Bill Rice and Dr. A.V. Henderson. There were many others too numerous to list.

After I met Dr. Henderson he invited me to preach twice at the great Detroit Baptist Temple in Pontiac, Michigan. It was an opportunity I really enjoyed.

The ministry of Baptist Tabernacle has been a blessing to so many people. The church has had the greatest preachers and singers in America in the pulpit. We have had great men like Dr. R.G. Lee, Dr. Lee Roberson, Dr. Jack Hudson, Dr. Tom Malone, and Dr. B.R.Lakin to name a few.

Many of the great ones have also served on our staff such as, Dr. J.C. House, Dr. Jimmy Hollingsworth, Dr. Orval Heath, Dr. Jim Thompson, Dr. Larry Gilliam, Dr. Morris Robe, Tommy Drewett, James Camp, Lloyd Reichen, James Murphy, Ray Guernsey and Randy Whitworth.

J.C. House

Dr. J.C. House and his wife, Doris, came to us after a bad experience with some church members. Discouragement is a tool of the devil and he needed a break from pastoring.

He was here only a short time before I asked him if he would pray about a small job in the church. His answer was, "I don't have to pray about it. I will take it." He went from that answer to being Co-Pastor.

Under his ministry here he brought the Sunday school to an average of over 600. Doris worked hard along with him visiting and teaching. These were good times in the history of the church.

Jimmy Combs

Dr. Jimmy Combs and his sweet wife, Jeri, have been very special friends through the years. He has been so interested in our work and always helpful in any way he could. Having worked with him closely I know his love for Christian Education. He has helped so many colleges through the years. His golden pen has written so many fine articles that have blessed my heart. He is a great man of God.

Billy Nichols

Dr. Billy Nichols, a successful evangelist and a member of Baptist Tabernacle, has retired from pastoring and gone into evangelism. He and his dear wife, Jeanette, are long time friends and we love them dearly.

Earl White

Dr. Earl White and his wife, Mary, retired as pastor of Shady Grove Baptist Church. He was also instructor in Baptist

Christian College, and meant a lot to us. He also had a class called "The Timothy Class" in his church where he taught young preachers.

Jerry Falwell

Dr. Jerry Falwell, very well known in Baptist ranks, has been a big influence to us. One time, he flew down at his own expense to speak at our church for a groundbreaking ceremony for a new building. He is a great example to young people and we appreciate him.

L.T. Chelette

L.T. Chelette and his wife, Gwen, are lay missionaries. They have spent much of their time helping me get where I am going. Since I have been disabled he goes many places with me, just to take care of me.

Dan Sawyer

Judge Dan Sawyer was our attorney at one time. He later became a judge and incidentally a dear friend to my family.

I have often said that Dan is like a brother to me because he has helped me in in ways only a brother can. The main thing I remember about Dan is how many times he lifted my spirits. We have had the privilege of having him in our home many times. No one has been more concerned about the pastor and our work as this judge.

I have always loved politics and liked to try to help those that were worthy. This is the case with Judge Dan

Sawyer. He is retired now but still comes to fellowship and worship. He once made the statement from our pulpit that I was the most dedicated man he had ever known. I did not feel worthy of the statement, but his generous comment meant a lot to me.

Richard Thompson

Richard Thompson, a graduate of Baptist Christian College, is one of our most successful students. After graduation he has worked in the State Department of Education, The Department of Corrections, and has been instrumental in raising funds for the college. Now he is living in Peurto Rico, where he is head of corrections.

He was at one time a staunch Church of Christ layman. Later, I had the privilege of winning and baptizing him at Baptist Tabernacle in Sibley, Louisiana. This was a great victory for the Lord.

Doyle Berry

Doyle Berry, a dear friend from Baton Rouge, called me several years ago asking me to assist in the gubernatorial campaign. He wanted me to host a meeting for Mike Foster, a relatively unknown candidate for governor of the state of Louisiana.

He told me all about the man and what he stood for. I was highly impressed with him and gladly accepted the task. Mike Foster was very low in the polls and most people told me he did not have a prayer of winning. My optimism took over and

I got busy. As more and more people saw what this man stood for, he began to show some gain in the polls and on election day we were elated when he was declared the winner.

William Smart

Dr. William Smart, who once taught at Baptist Christian College, is a good, long-time friend of ours. He has been working at Louisiana Baptist University recruiting students. His former wife Nelta was the first principal of BCA.

Mike Foster

Governor Mike Foster appreciated my help and asked me to lead the prayer at his Inauguration Ceremony. The ceremony was held on one of the coldest days in the history of Louisiana. Edith purchased me a new black topcoat, and we went proudly to the Inauguration, one of the highlights of my ministry.

Governor Foster has been one of the most popular governors for two terms now, and people have asked me many times to contact him to assist them in different ways. He has always taken the time to respond to my request and has repeatedly tried to help me.

One of the highlights of my life was to get to duck hunt with the governor and his bodyguard. I joked when telling people that the bodyguard was there to protect me and not the governor.

Once I took Judge Sawyer and Wayne Waddell, a state representative, to the Governor's Mansion for dinner and an overnight stay. Breakfast and a Bible Study followed next morning. Judge Sawyer commented on what a wonderful governor as well as spiritual leader Mike Foster had proved to be.

On several occasions, Dr. Bobby Burnett, former Chairman of The Louisiana Baptist Bible Fellowship, and I, asked the governor to host an overnight stay in the Governor's Mansion with dinner and breakfast served. All of the preachers thoroughly enjoyed this. It is nice to have the honor of being personal friends with the governor and his lovely wife, Alice. We thank God for this wonderful man.

Helen Sutton

I have had so many wonderful friends and influences, which helped me along life's way. I remember Mrs. Helen Sutton, who was my schoolteacher in the first and second grade in Sibley. I remember how this dear Christian lady influenced me to want to be my best and first taught me how to read and write.

Later on in the years, it was this same sweet school teacher who would witness to me many times. She would say, "Jimmy ,are you coming to church on Sunday?" I can still hear that voice, even though many times I did not heed the call. It lingers in my heart even now, how much she cared for me. It was also this lady who taught me not to do wrong.

One day, while sitting in her classroom, I kept noticing a small chalky looking dog, and another dog with her pups on the windowsill. The more I looked at those little dogs, the more I wanted them.

Right before the bell rang at the end of the day, I took those little dogs, put them in my pocket and started home. It was then I heard a voice behind me calling, "Jimmy, Jimmy!"

I turned around and, as you have probably guessed, it was Mrs. Sutton. She asked what I had in my pockets. At first I fibbed and said, "Nothing." She then checked my pockets and pulled the little dogs out. Then she lifted my trouser leg and spanked me.

I'll never forget that day, it taught me the invaluable lesson of why you should not steal, a lesson that I have remembered to this day.

I have often asked people if they would rather be a half-hearted whole-wit or a whole hearted half-wit.

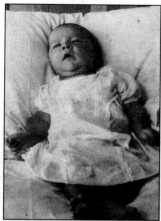

Jim Tharpe - one month old

Bonnie Lee and Jimmy Tharpe

Edith at 16 years

Jimmy Tharpe at 17 years

Mr. and Mrs. M.A. Moore -
Edith's parents

Mr. and Mrs. L.H. Tharpe -
Jimmy's parents

Newlyweds - 1950

Family as it was when we moved to Shreveport

When all the kids were home

Clayton Weaver, Mayor
Fant, Dr. Tharpe, and
Dr. Collins.
    Ground Breaking

First building at Baptist Tabernacle - white two story, Charles McBride - Deacon with pastor

Early days of Academy

Baptist Tabernacle and congregation

Pastor Baptizing Mother, Father, and Wife for Trinity

Ground breaking ceremony
crowd for auditorium

Very early days. Preaching at Webster
Parist Jal

Happy Pastor at his desk

Pastor in his office in Baptist Tabernacle

Pastor, went musical at graduation outdoor banquet

Graduation, left to right: Dr. Tharpe Phil Martin, David Peterson and Johnny Ramsey

Baseball team in 1951 Jimmy Tharpe on bottom

First National Championship BCC Baseball in Kansas May 1991
Roger Tharpe, coach

Big Bear and Pastor, which is which?

J.G. Tharpe and hunting site in
Colorado

Ready to shoot!
Where's the game?

Preaching the Word!

Bill Kincaid, In the new building

Lash Larue and Pastor Tharpe

Enjoying a Fish Fry at Dorcheat - Pastor, Mr. Cummings, Louie Grafton
and Fletcher Caldwell

Captain Tharpe
driving houseboat

Our children enjoying the
cruise to the Bahamas

Pastor and Mrs. Homan on houseboat on Dorcheat

Pastor at his camp on beautiful Bayou Dorcheat

Beautiful Bayou Dorcheat

Good friends -
Hollingsworths, Chelettes, Tharpes, and Knights

"First Cruise"
Jimmy and Edith Tharpe, Don and Louise Chelette

1977 Holy Land trip

Jimmy, George, and Jack

Pastor and Gov. Treen

Family
Portrait
'60s

Governor,
Pastor, and
John
Rawlings

Governor
Foster
receiving
honorary
degree

Governor's Inauguration

Good times
Betty Lawrence, Norma Boyd and Edith

Billy Francis, Jimmy, Edith, and Dale Robertson

Pastor and friends in Mexico on mission trip

Edith, Jimmy, and
Bro House

Pastor and Bro.
J.C. House

Dr. John Rawlings
at Tabernacle

First new car - given by church

Another new car

40th Anniversary
First Deacons and wives: Charles McBride and his
wife Helen, Mary and L.G. Morris, Roland Liles,
L .A. Grafton and Jimmy Tharpe

Busy, Busy, Busy

Two happy people,
Jimmy Tharpe and
Clayton Weaver

Tharpe receiving Hall
of Fame awarded by
Dr. Jack Hall
of Ft. Worth

Dr. Mike Landry and Family

New Church building and museum here

Grand Children
Children's Children are the crown of old men - Prov. 17:6

Winning basketball team, Coach Phil Martin on right

Pastor receiving a gift from Joy club Maxine Schepp

Pastor and "Lil' Gene Murphy

Pastor and Larry Norrell

Preaching at Baptist Tabernacle

Pastor and some boys from "Boys Home"

Welcome home from hospital
- Jimmy and family

Homecoming from hospital. Ed, Norma
& Jimmy, Edith

One of the
beautiful
automobiles
given
Tharpes by
the church

52nd Anniversary limousine

Jimmy and Edith walking toward the sunset

CHAPTER 6

BCC, BCA, LBU

Baptist Christian College

A great vision came to me while attending Centenary College…a vision that started in an odd way.

I remember one professor saying that he was certain nobody could believe that the Genesis account of creation was literal. He skeptically groaned, "Come on, now!"

I attempted to explain it to him. He said, "If I want a sermon, I'll come to your church and hear one." I liked the idea of preaching to him, but I knew I couldn't hold my breath waiting for that day to come.

Another lady in the classroom said, "Jesus did not walk on the water. That's just good reading." I was stunned to hear her say this. She was a Sunday school teacher in a large Methodist church.

127

On another occasion they were discussing the television show, Peyton Place. The question was asked, "What is good literature?" The class was asked for their opinion.

When it was my turn to speak, I said, "Good literature is the word of God, and I love reading it. It contains all kinds of literature." The professor again made the statement that there would be no preaching in this class.

Still, I did have some good professors there that helped me many times. One was Dr. W. Pledger. I loved him dearly. He was a kind and wonderful man.

It was in class at Centenary that I prayed for God to send someone to build a fundamental school after the patterns of proper teaching and doctrines. God didn't send anyone at that time. Finally, I believed He had laid it on my heart to build Baptist Christian College.

We started in a little room in the educational building with donated help. W.F. Mears, Dr. Billy McCormack, Dr. John R. Bryant, and so many others gave of their time to help us. Dr. Roy Norton kindly did his part in helping with the college. He even helped in naming the school, Baptist Christian College.

Many great men helped in building our college. Dr. Corbett Mask, who meant so much in the early days, was at that time vice-president of Baptist Christian College. He was a great fundraiser. The sweet memory of him will always be in my heart even though he has gone on to be with the Lord. At one time, Dr. Mask had been chaplain of the State Senate of Arkansas for eight years. He built many churches and was a dynamic preacher.

Baptist Christian College was organized in 1961 and was one of Baptist Tabernacle's first ministries. Many thousands of students were trained there in Bible, education, and business administration. They came from all over the nation as well as foreign countries too.

The college was founded over forty-two years ago when dedicated Christian educators, church leaders, and students came together to fulfill a need which they discerned the Lord had called them to fulfill. They worked together with others to develop the institution. We wanted the college to take care of the heart as well as the intellect. We wanted to have a dedicated Christian college that would uphold the principles of God, and that it did.

During the first three years we prepared students for ministerial and other church related vocations. In 1964, a degree in elementary education was added in response to the need for Christian elementary teachers to serve in Christian schools.

In the fall of 1967, the Louisiana State Department of Education recognized and approved the elementary education program, allowing a student completing all requirements of the program to receive a Louisiana certification in elementary education. In 1971, we started offering courses in secondary education and obtained State approval for certification in social studies and physical education.

In January of 1986, I became Chancellor and Dr. Phil Martin was installed as the second president. In 1990, we began the task of obtaining accreditation from TRACS and received candidacy status. This allowed us to apply for Title IV programs for federal financial aid to our students.

In 1993, the Board of Regents of Louisiana licensed us. All of this required piles of records, money, etc. We even applied for approval from the Southern Association, which was harder than all the rest, but we were never able to obtain that accreditation. To our credit, many of our graduates have experienced high levels of success in their chosen vocations.

The college grew in numbers as a result of being able to receive federal funds and all of the programs benefited. The secondary education program was very good for physical education programs. This gave us good athletes as well as physical education teachers.

BCC was known as the "Cradle of Coaches." It virtually trained hundreds of men and women in the field of coaching and teaching. Our athletes have won State championships, produced nine "All Americans" in basketball, six in baseball, and three in football. BCC won four national championships in baseball, some of them back to back, and placed third, two times in basketball.

The physical education teachers we trained are coaching and teaching all over and we are very proud of them, as we are many of our alumni. We have had several of our elementary teachers named "Teacher of the Year" in Louisiana.

Dr. Phil Martin recently said, "Thousands of students were trained to be teachers, coaches, counselors, preachers, and professionals because of the visions and ministries of Dr. Jimmy and Dr. Edith Tharpe." Many are still teaching today in the private as well as the Christian sector.

My wife, Dr. Edith Tharpe, was Dean of Education for many years and takes great joy in the many teachers throughout the state and around the world who were certified through Baptist Christian College.

The main campus facilities included the following:

The Education Building, a modern structure contained the Office of the President, the administrative offices of the Department of Education, the Academic Affairs Office, the Registrar's Office, the Business Office, a meeting/dining room and kitchen facility for informal dining on campus, the Admissions Office, the Financial Aid Office, the Counseling and Testing Center, as well as classrooms and other meeting rooms.

The Business Education Building, contained classrooms, the computer center, support services and the administrative office of Student Services.

The Library, which held thousands of volumes as well as the audiovisual and video equipment, also contained reading and conference areas, and the administrative offices of the library.

The Health and Physical Education Complex consisted of a gymnasium, exercise facility, and athletic offices adjacent to the football and baseball fields.

College Hall was a multipurpose building full of classrooms and offices.

The Auditorium contained not only the main complex, with seating for over 1200, but also the administrative offices of the Department of Biblical Studies and Christian

Education.

Various other multipurpose buildings included the Fellowship Building, Maintenance Building and the Print Shop.

Though we were so happy to receive federal funding, it turned out to cause our downfall. We got too ambitious and opened up schools for inmates in Louisiana prisons. As it ended, the US Department of Education cut off the funding for these and left us holding the bag to pay the teachers and all the other expenses we had incurred. The same thing happened to our off-campus programs, such as Leesville, Alexandria, and Winnfield.

Unfortunately, after 35 years of operation, extra fast growth and other problems caused Baptist Christian College to close it's doors, bringing to an end the ministry that had helped so many people in so many ways. In August of 1996, we graduated our last group of students. We had to find other colleges who would accept those students who were lower classmates.

Baptist Christian Academy

In 1964, Baptist Christian Academy was founded. We enjoyed twenty-four beautiful years with that school. We had a high of 636 students at one time. The first principals were Ruby Fitzgerald (now deceased), John Byrd (the mean old bird that believed in corporal punishment), and Nelta Smart (who didn't believe in it at all). Nelta was there when Judge Dan Sawyer became active in our Parent-Teacher Organization.

We started off with just some of the elementary grades, first through eighth. We later added middle school and high school. The school was founded on my belief that we needed to provide Christian Education to our children, and we opened this opportunity to others in the community.

Baptist Christian Academy preceded the integration of our public schools, but this was not what prompted our existence. However, when integration was ordered, our halls were lined with crying, pleading parents looking to place their children who they had already pulled out of school. If memory serves me right, we were the only Baptist school in town. There were a few parochial, and one non-denominational school in the area. Every school was bombarded at the time.

They came to us from every walk of life. There were doctors, lawyers, judges, and families of means. If we would take their children, they promised to live by our rules and comply in every way. Some offered to endow us to meet the financial demands that would be incurred in expanding, and would help build buildings if necessary.

After a year of weeding the tares from the wheat, we had a good school, and for years maintained a strong and healthy enrollment. Then, one by one, new schools sprang up, and many who had come begging left to go to schools more conveniently located. Many who left were among the founders of these newly created schools.

The State of Louisiana and the Louisiana Independent School Association (known as LISA) had accredited our academy. LISA provided private schools the opportunity to participate in athletics statewide, and it was a good thing. We were to be reckoned with in all sports....football, basketball, baseball, and softball.

Our greatest and fondest win was over First Baptist right here in Shreveport. The night our basketball team won that game in our gym gave the whole school a boost. On one side were our fans, and on the other were the doctors, lawyers, and judges that had pulled their kids out of our school to start their own.

Don't get me wrong, we were not mean spirited! They had good schools, just a little more liberal than BCA who was from the other side of the track (in their opinion). Thus, we were pleased to show so well in athletics.

Over the years, public school enrollment settled down. Parents were increasingly tolerant of integration practices and in most cases the students didn't mind going to public schools. It was much more affordable than the cost of a private school education and enrollment in all private schools was diminished.

First Baptist dropped back to K-8th grade, as did Calvary Baptist, and many of the private schools not connected to a church closed their doors. We lasted a long long time and sadly, joined the ranks of those who gave in to the diminishing preference in Christian education. We graduated our last class in 1988.

Today, all over town, Edith and I meet people who had children and grandchildren who attended our school. They come up to tell us how much they appreciate the education that they received.

Louisiana Baptist University

Louisiana Baptist University, formerly Baptist Christian University, was established in 1973 and has been in operation for thirty years. It was founded as a graduate school completely separate from Baptist Christian College.

Dr. Neal Weaver has been the president for many years and has done a wonderful job. Dr. Jimmy Combs serves as provost of Louisiana Baptist Theological Seminary and Dr. Fred Moody is Dean. As a part of its significant growth and development, the University instituted the Seminary division in 1988. We now have over 1200 students in this one school.

Dr. Weaver is a very close friend as well as an outstanding preacher and educator. While I thank God for others who served before Dr. Weaver, he has surely brought the university to heights we have never known. Others could not work full-time at the job. Dr. Weaver has accepted this as the will of God for his life.

We are very proud of Dr. Weaver, Dr. Sandra Cory who is executive vice-president, and others on the staff who have done such a good job. The majority of the students are off campus and use the Directed Individual Study (DIS) form of learning.

The purpose for which Louisiana Baptist University was established is to provide graduate educational opportunities for pastors and Christian workers so they can earn their graduate degrees and continue their work at their churches at the same time. From a modest beginning, LBU has steadily developed into an important institution in Christian higher education.

For three decades it has been our privilege to train thousands of pastors, missionaries, Christian educators and business people who now literally serve around the world in many nations and cultures, while maintaining professional excellence in their Christian lifestyles.

LBU has been a pioneer in distance education. We are now moving rapidly into the technology age in order to be able to train even more students at remote locations. In developing this program we have adopted the best methodologies and technologies of other outstanding schools such as University of Maryland, Liberty University, Nova University and The Union Institute.

Our desire is to provide the best in both academic and spiritual training. Many universities offer excellent academic programs that challenge the mind, but we feel that, as a Christian institution, we must also be committed to building the students faith.

Baptist Christian University was asked to change its name in 1994 when Baptist Christian College was attempting to attain accreditation from Transnational Association of Christian Schools (TRACS). The name Louisiana Baptist University was adopted so there would be no conflict between schools. The new name has been well received by current students, alumni, and appropriate agencies.

We had leased a floor of the five-story Centrum building, which we have used for several years on Hollywood Avenue. The facilities were first class with glass elevators and all the amenities you would expect in a modern office building. In 2002, Louisiana Baptist University decided to purchase a building on I-20 in an area which is growing rapidly. The new 12,500 square-foot building is located right in the center of West Shreveport. The remodeling is now complete and we have taken occupancy. It is a beautiful location and is a very positive step forward.

Louisiana Baptist University and Theological Seminary is privileged to have thirteen College or Seminary presidents among its alumni. It is a honor that these outstanding educators selected LBU/LBTS to earn their doctorate and they are doing great, which can partly be attributed to their education. Some of our other outstanding students are:

Dr. Deborah Yow

Dr. Chuck Missler

Dr. Grant Jeffrey

Dr. Billy Hamm

Dr. Terry Lyles

Dr. Kim Alan Beckham

Dr. Bob Gray

Dr. Duke Chi

Dr. George Flanagan

Dr. Jimmy DeYoung

We always had a joint graduation and one of the outstanding events of the year for everybody was graduation day. We always made the day memorable by planning an impressive commencement ceremony in addition to special events.

Since so many students were from out of the area, we had what we call, "A Taste of Louisiana," featuring several Cajun and Creole foods. This was held outdoors on the campus for lack of another place large enough to take care of the crowd. I was apologizing for this at our first outdoor banquet and; many people said to me, "Always do it outdoors. Never go inside again because it is absolutely perfect."

We had live Cajun music, boats full of shrimp, crawfish, jambalaya, fried catfish, other choice seafoods, and wonderful desserts. It only rained one year at graduation, and I do have to admit, that was a miserable day.

LBU is still doing this Cajun feast, one of the highlights of graduation. We had small graduations in the early years, but since Dr. Weaver took on the leadership, he has increased the number of students dramatically. LBU/LBTS is averaging around 200 graduates annually and has been blessed to have many outstanding graduation speakers. The speakers include Attorney General John Ashcroft, Author Tim LaHaye and a host of great preachers and educators.

One of the most exciting parts of our graduation is meeting graduates from all the foreign countries. Some years there can be as many as ten (10) different nationalities who come to Shreveport to take part in the graduation. There are always 25 or 30 graduates from Korea and Japan. The Korean ladies are always beautiful in their traditional Korean dresses. Many of the students can speak very little English so it is an adventure just trying to communicate.

CHAPTER 7

PHILOSOPHY AND EDUCATION

Most people would say that I have a strange philosophy of life. I would rather shoot big and miss than never to shoot at all. I have always been an optimist and believed in the power of positive thinking.

There were two men in jail with different views. When they looked through the bars, one saw the mud, the other saw the stars. I have often asked people if they would rather be a half-hearted whole-wit or a wholehearted half-wit.

The Bible says that without a vision the people perish. To encourage and motivate people is one of my main joys in life. I can honestly say that I do not love money or material things.

Once, while preaching in South Texas, a music director

admired a tan jacket I was wearing. He said the cleaners had lost one of his just like it. When the service was over, I pulled my coat off and gave it to him. He was shocked that I would do this.

Later, my wife scolded me for giving him the jacket because my daughter, Debbye, had given it to me as a gift. I told her that God would give me another one. When I told Debbye, who is very much like me, she went out and bought me another jacket, a beautiful brick red color.

A few months passed and a box arrived for me in the mail. It was my tan coat, with a letter inside from that man telling me that his coat had been found and he was returning mine. I happily told my wife that I now had two coats because I had given one away. This is the way it has been for me with money and material things.

To my wife's dismay, many times I have given my entire paycheck to families less fortunate than my own. But I knew, as she knew, you can never out give God. I am still willing to live simply from hand to mouth. That is, God's hand to my mouth. He has been so good to us through the years. I have never had a savings account and try to keep my money in circulation. God has bestowed unlimited blessings on us.

We now live in a $200,000 dollar home that the church paid off as a gift on the day of my retirement. My wife owns a Buick, an inheritance from her parents, and we drive a beautiful Lincoln given to us by the kind, loving members of Baptist Tabernacle. He blessed us with a camp on Bayou Dorcheat, and our biggest blessing, six beautiful children and their spouses. To date, we have six children, twenty grandchildren and eleven great-grandchildren. How much more could God bless a fisherman's son from Sibley?

I have always been a visionary, "a dreamer." The Bible teaches that people perish without a vision. The church has always been gracious to follow me in most of these visions, therefore, many wonderful things have been accomplished.

Forgiveness is one characteristic of a Christian that seems very difficult to master. One desire of mine through the years was for my people to view me as a person who forgives quickly and easily. The Bible says much about forgiveness. The Lord said in His prayer, "Forgive us our trespasses as we forgive those who trespass against us."

I remember when I first became serious about my school career. I went to Dr. L.L. Clover and discussed it with him. I told him I wanted to keep my railroad job and preach on the side, but that I was very interested in getting an education. He chuckled and said, "Son, let me give you some good advice. You know God has called you to preach and if God can feed the Israelites out in the wilderness he can surely take care of a preacher and his family. If you are not willing to eat peas and cornbread and make a few sacrifices to train for the ministry, then you are not worth the salt that goes in your bread."

I was very angry but I wouldn't say so. He drove a beautiful car and lived in a very nice brick home. I assumed a man who could say this, having no children of his own, must have been lacking in compassion. However, I took his advice and it turned my life around. I enrolled in school and was very happy studying God's word.

I had been a student of Louisiana Missionary Baptist Institute and Seminary in Minden, Louisiana. I had studied the word of God from eight until twelve every day of the week. We had forty-four students in the school by the end of the first year.

The school started with just two students, Leroy Mitchell and me, in Brother Clover's home. Brother Clover taught us great doctrines of the church and baptism, and some I have held to through the years have supported my ministry. I will always appreciate that seminary.

The Hebrew, Greek, and other things they taught have helped me considerably. Even though I went to five colleges, I credit my Bible knowledge to that seminary and the kind people who taught us there so faithfully. I helped to raise money in the mission rallies to help in buying the property there and building the seminary. I felt a part of it then as I do today. My brother, George, attended there for a year before he surrendered to preach.

After I finished my Seminary one day I came in and said to Edith, "I am going to enroll at Centenary College to further my education." She said, "You have been in school for years. Don't you think you have had enough?" I told her I felt like God was leading me to do this.

I enrolled in the evening division at Centenary and for over three years attended night classes. I later transferred to East Texas Baptist College in Marshall, Texas where Dr. Bennett was President. I remember one semester I could not pay my tuition. I had to go to Dr. Bennett's office and tell him that I was working very hard to get my education but did not have the money to enroll at the moment.

He just smiled and said, "We'll help you get enrolled." He allowed me to pay it later in the semester. He was a very gracious man and I was thankful for his help.

I later attended Trinity College in Clearwater, Florida, where I received a Masters Degree signed by the great President, Dr. T.W. Watson. They had a special program and for two summers I attended. I stayed in the dormitories, met wonderful people, and heard some great professors.

This is the school that Billy Graham once attended. It was then called Florida Baptist Institute. The graduation was held in Graham Garden Sanctuary, a very beautiful place. I cherish that memory. As I recall, there were forty-four students in Billy's class and at the time he did not know the will of God for his life.

I read the prophecy in the yearbook and saw the young preacher, Billy. I even read his transcript. He had moved there from Bob Jones University. Dr. Bob Jones had written a letter to Dr. Watson informing him that two young men would seek admission to his school. He said that one would not amount to much but that the other one, Billy, had great prospects if his feet were held to the fire. Dr. Watson stopped and laughed as he read me the letter. He said, "We put Billy's heart to the fire." It was that year that Billy gave a donation of several thousand dollars to Trinity College.

Years later I enrolled in National Christian University

where Dr. Stoval was President. Several good friends enrolled along with me and received their degrees from NCU. I received my PhD. in Psychology. Some of my classmates were Dr. J.C. House, Dr. Morris Robe, Dr. Billy McCormack, Dr. Perry Purtle, and Dr. O.P. Bazar. We had such great fellowship and I count them all dear friends to this day. I remember the night that we graduated because it was that night that Mr. Melvin Mund, who was heard over the radio for years, received an Honorary Doctorate in the same service.

Edith Tharpe

I must say a few words about my sweet wife who has been such a great blessing to me since the day I met her. Words could never express what she means to my heart.

She is the mother of six wonderful children. She is also a great lady of faith, love, and concern for people, especially her family. She is the very heart of our family.

Her children all arise and call her "Blessed." Her husband will praise her at the gates as the Bible says. She has been a wonderful encouragement throughout my ministry. Many times, when I have been at my lowest, a few words of encouragement would completely lift me up.

She has been a loving and faithful wife, supporting me in everything I did. She has even supported my many visions throughout the years, although sometimes she may not have felt as strongly about them as I did.

Edith first graduated from Baptist Christian College with a Bachelors Degree in Education. She then drove one hundred fifty miles roundtrip to Northwestern State University several days a week to earn a Masters Degree in 1972 and a Doctorate of Education in 1976. She received special recognition during the graduation.

I remember many times she would come home weeping because things weren't going right. I would try to encourage her. Even though it was sometimes a struggle, she continued to accomplish her goal. The Doctor Of Education Degree she earned was a large asset to Baptist Christian College and has helped hundreds of people further their education over the years.

When I think of Edith, I think of her as a loving mother, homemaker, excellent cook, and a counselor to church members and college students from all over the world, but mostly to her children. She wrote her dissertation on "Teacher Morale." It was an excellent piece of work and later there was an article in a national magazine featuring a section of her dissertation. I will never forget when she showed me her name in that magazine.

The night she graduated, I sat in the balcony with our family, in awe of the task she had performed. When the ceremony was over I made my way to her. I congratulated her with a hug and a kiss. She looked up at me and said, "You know I did this for you," even though we both knew she did it for the Lord. I wept tears of pride and joy. She has done so many things for me, for our work, and for Almighty God through the years. She is loved and respected by the members of Baptist Tabernacle.

*I have always been a visionary, "a dreamer." The Bible
teaches that people perish without a vision.*

CHAPTER 8

HUNTING EXPERIENCES

My experience in hunting has been extraordinary. It goes all the way back to when my father bought me a "Long Tom" shotgun. It was taller than I was at the time, and I know now I should not have been hunting at my age.

My grandfather, Center Crump, had a cute little dog whose name was Buster. He was good at running rabbits and treeing any animal you could imagine. Everyone loved him dearly, especially my grandfather who we called Popoo.

One morning, I took several people hunting. Buster jumped a rabbit and the rabbit ran under a log. Immediately they began to shout, "Jim! Kill the rabbit when it comes out from under the log!" When I saw the rabbit, I shot at once. The shot killed the rabbit, but it also killed Buster.

That was one sad day in my life. I knew I had to face Granny and Popoo Crump and give them the terrible news of Buster's death. Billy Crump, my cousin, began to cry and said, "You've shot ole Buster." Ducie, our good black friend who was along for the hunt, quickly took flight. He often laughed and told me he would never go hunting with me again.

When we reached Popoo, he was working in his shop. I began to weep as I told him the news. All Papoo said was, "Well, it couldn't be helped." When Granny heard what had happened, her reaction was, "Us cook this rabbit and eat it." She always used "us" as a subject because of her mother tongue. So they were not too upset.

The duck hunting experience I remember most was at the age of seventeen. I had gone squirrel hunting with Tracy McLemore, who married my first cousin, Alys Tharpe. At the end of the day, we found ourselves facing two game wardens. The problem was we had six ducks that were illegal because the season was not open.

The flight of ducks had come in that day while we were squirrel hunting and we could not resist. I was not a Christian at the time. The day of the trial is one I will never forget.

I stood in my father's suit (that did not fit) wearing a necktie that was choking me. Tracy and I each received a twenty-five dollar fine and a five year suspended sentence. I can assure you, it was more than five years before I could look a duck in the eye again. It was a lesson well learned. Standing before an earthly judge gave me some insight as to how it might be standing before the Great Judge.

Years later, on one occasion, we were doing mission work in Mexico. When our work was done Brother Mike Patterson, the missionary, invited us to stay another day. He promised to take us "sail fishing." We gladly accepted the invitation. The next morning Don, Louise, Edith and I set out on our big sail fishing adventure. We hoped to catch at least two sailfish. Brother Don graciously told me to go ahead and try to catch the first one.

There was a small one that got on the line and quickly got off. After lunch we had a big strike from a large sailfish. Edith saw the fish approaching the hook and line, its big fin sticking up out of the water. We saw it when it took the bait. We took pictures as we landed him, which took thirty minutes. I was wringing wet with perspiration. Our wives were very excited. We prayed it would be a good one and it was.

Brother Don landed his fish and I prayed it would be smaller than mine. After the big weigh-in event, God answered my prayer but not by much. My fish was nine feet long and weighed one hundred thirty pounds. Brother Don's fish weighed one hundred twenty-two pounds and was four inches shorter than mine. I rubbed it in on him, but had he not been so gracious to let me go first, I may not have gotten one at all.

Another good fishing trip was on the Gulf of Mexico. L. G. Morris, Wilburn Scott, their wives, Betty and Mary, and Edith and I, went out from Cameron, Louisiana to fish for red snapper. We caught over six hundred fish. It was a lot of work but sure was fun.

The main highlight of my hunting career was the "Bear Hunt in Alaska." Brother Don Chelette and I had another great time on this trip.

Brother Les Zerbe, a missionary, had a plane and graciously took us to the big moose country to hunt for moose and bear. I thought I saw a big moose but Brother Zerbe took the binoculars and said, "No, that is a big grizzly bear coming down that mountain." I said, "Let's go after him." Brother Don said, "I will wait here. Brother Les told him that sometimes a bear would circle around so Don decided to go with us.

Can you imagine that I, who is afraid of a little dog, had no fear of a big grizzly bear? We began to stalk the bear. Brother Les told us to keep our guns off safety and be ready to shoot at any time. We spread out a few feet apart and began to hunt the bear. He was evidently hiding from us.

All of the sudden, I saw Les raise his arm up high in the air. I looked right in front of me and saw the big grizzly sitting on his hind legs looking from left to right. I said, "Les, I am going to take him." We had been talking like you normally would because it sounds like a strange caribou to the bear. I shot and the bear went down. Les said, "I've never seen a bear go down so quickly." I knew he was going to die because I put another bullet right through his heart. He wallowed around a little while in the bush and we could not see him.

Brother Les said, "We will circle around and if the bear attacks me you will have to shoot him off. I would rather be killed by a gun than by the bear." Of course, we were very careful and would never shoot wildly. He circled the bear, poked him with the end of his gun barrel, and said, "He is a dead bear." I stood watch while they skinned the bear. The hide weighed over one hundred pounds and we had to carry it five miles. It was quite an ordeal. We got back to camp one hour before darkness set in.

On the return trip we had no communications when flying between the mountains. We were afraid we might lose our lives. We had hit snow and ice and visibility was limited. Les was a great pilot. He stayed in the pattern of the little riverbed below him. If he lost sight of it he would ask if we could see it. At one point he said, "I am going to try to make it to a certain place and go almost straight up. Hopefully we will see a little light shining and I will know where I am in the midst of all this snow and sleet."

When we reached a high enough altitude we could see a bright light that was definitely a welcome sight. We all rejoiced because our prayers had been answered. We then saw a flickering light, and Les had to bring the plane in sideways. It then just dropped on the runway where they had a rescue-meeting place in the woods. I was so thankful, thinking mainly that if we crashed I could not make it home to brag to my family and church about the bear. I often tease people by saying, "Have I told you the story of my bear?" One man said, "Yes, Brother Tharpe, about six times."

I can also remember the moose hunt in Canada, L.G. Morris, Wilburn Scott, Don Chelette and I went on. Scott and Morris killed two big elk. It took the entire time of the trip to get all that meat processed and ready to go back home.

Later, L.G.'s son, Dennis, killed a big moose. Canada was a wonderful place. I always had the desire to hunt in Canada and Alaska, and God answered those prayers.

For many years, I had the privilege of directing leases in the great state of Texas. It was there we had many wonderful times camping out. One of the fun times was when Don Edwards had a picture of a deer drawn on a cardboard box. We used it to play jokes on the preachers. I will never forget Johnny Ramsey arriving late for one hunt.

We began to bait him, telling him there was an exotic wild animal out there. We began to drive around the lease to let him spot the "deer." He got out of the vehicle thinking he had spotted a big deer. He shot eleven times, until he ran out of shells.

The boys were laughing in the back of the truck. He came and got himself two more shells. I told him, "Slip up a little closer, Johnny." He slipped up closer only to discover he had been set up. He looked at me and said, "I almost cursed before I had a heart attack." Brother Don later put some little beeps on the machine that sounded like ugly words, but in all respect to Brother Ramsey, he had not said anything wrong.

The next year we fooled him again by telling him we would kill a jack rabbit so big he could make a "jackalope" out of it. The boys had gone to town and purchased some string. Don Edwards then took some skin from a jackrabbit and placed it over a roller skate. It made something that looked exactly like the rabbit himself.

It was dark and Johnny was in a good position to shoot.

We said, "Johnny, is that a rabbit?" He began to shoot at what he thought was a rabbit. From behind, where they could not be seen, the boys began to pull the string. Johnny began to shoot at the rabbit. He would shoot and the boys would pull. He shot at that rabbit time and time again until he realized that once again, he was had.

When you dish it out, you have to learn to take it. I am afraid this goes for me as well. One day they put a five-foot long rattlesnake Don Edwards had killed in my stand. They were all eager to help me get into my stand. They had the rattlesnake there waiting for me. They had posed it all coiled up, as if ready to strike.

I climbed on my stand and looked right into the face of that rattlesnake. I will never forget that feeling. I said, "Whoa!" and then fell backwards, landing right on a big rock. They asked if I was hurt, and I quickly told them I was not. Of course I was hurt, but nothing could have made me admit it to them at that moment. I crawled to a tree and tried to find a place to curl up and die. I would bail out again today if I tried to climb into a stand and looked into the eyes of a coiled rattler. I had to take some of my own medicine that day.

Another highlight of our hunting career was a trip we took to Canada to hunt for moose. We had a guide go ahead of us. Don Edwards had planted the moose he painted and also an elk. They both looked extremely real. He set them up on stakes in some bushes. Three cameras were on him when Brother Ramsey tried to shoot at the prize moose. Finally he heard the clicking of the camera and knew he had been fooled yet again. We then went to the moose and made him stand beside it and take his picture with his moose. We all had a big laugh. Even Johnny had to laugh.

My two sons, Jim and Roger, used to hunt with us in Texas. I remember one occasion when I placed Roger on a stand. I told him that if by chance he killed anything, the others and I would come back and help him dress it. I happened to have three tags for that morning. When I returned, Roger had killed three bucks, and had a fourth in his sites. He shot but the gun snapped. These are some of the blessings that come from having your boys hunt with you through the years.

I have been privileged to have a family that always enjoyed hunting. Some of them now have leases and camps. Recently, I had the good fortune to be able to kill a ten by ten elk. This was made possible for me by Phil and Jonathan Martin: my son-in-law and grandson. I am financially indebted to them for all the wonderful fishing and hunting trips I recently enjoyed. They even had the meat dressed, frozen, and placed into my freezer. I appreciate everything they do for me.

Fletcher Caldwell has been a wonderful friend who takes me to his family deer lease. He has fixed a stand for me so that I can get out of the truck, take a few steps, and be in my stand. He has supplied me with everything I could need in my stand, including food and even a heater. Being handicapped, I would not have the opportunity to hunt, without special help, and I thank God he provided that for me. We haven't killed anything but time, but we always have a great time when we go.

CHAPTER 9

NEW BUILDING /NEW PASTOR

As in so many cities, changes occur over the years. Our church location and neighborhood had declined and became a place where crime and drugs were rampant. Our older people were afraid to come to church at night, so we had to consider moving out.

We put the building up for sale, but it was hard to find a buyer because we had so many buildings that were designed for a school and church. But, we finally were able to sell it to the Zion Baptist Church, a church which had many ministries so it was ideal for them.

The week we moved was a very sad occasion. To give up the place we loved so much, with so many memories, was very difficult. The first place we moved was to an upstairs banquet room of the Pelican Inn. There was no space for Sunday School, choir, etc. We even had to use an electric keyboard because we couldn't get a piano up the stairs. This was a good temporary place, but it was not suitable for older people.

We were waiting to start our new building program on the new property. We moved again to Kingston Road where we rented a part of a church, but it also was very small. We made out the best we could until we could get our new buildings ready. We were very happy to get into our new building. It is so beautiful and comfortable.

Mr. Fletcher Caldwell was our building superintendent and did a really good job. My very talented nephew, Dennis Tharpe, was also instrumental in helping us finish some of the areas. Dennis worked very hard to make sure we had everything ready for our first big day.

At that time, Mr. Weaver had taken over for me since this all occurred after my stroke. He made sure that our building was completed. As soon as we got in the new building, our church began to grow again. I was still disabled and my preachers in the church took over and rotated preaching for all the services. As you can see, it was a very difficult time. But, God blessed anyway! Our church called Brother Gary Wilson as a co-pastor during the time I was still disabled.

In July 2002, the church called Brother Mike Landry as pastor. He had served as co-pastor in 1993, but had been called to the mission field. Brother Mike had been in Romania, ministering to those people, when our church called him as pastor.

All through the years, God bestowed many blessings upon our ministries. Baptist Tabernacle has had several co-pastors and I thank God for every one of them and what they have done for our church. Dr. Orval Heath, Dr. J.C. House, under whose leadership the church excelled in all facets, Dr. Chuck Stevenson, Dr. Mike Landry, and Dr. Gary Wilson, all served in this capacity.

I am still indebted to a great host of staff workers and secretaries who made my job easier and who became a tremendous blessing to the ministries of Baptist Tabernacle. Elaine Robe, Georgia Bryan, Nell Reeves, Lois Murphy, Betty Lawrence, Melinda Waller, Fredia Edwards, Linda Weaver, Sandy Edwards, and Debbie Adams served as the secretaries for the church. Connie Landry is the current secretary. These ladies helped me so very much. Without them, my ministry would have been less successful. They worked hard at their job and were the first seen or heard by persons coming to my office. They had to smile when they didn't feel like it and listen to lots of tales.

Some of my staff had longevity so I want to mention a few who were so faithful and loyal. I am indebted to these men, especially Brother Clayton Weaver. Brother Clayton was so kind and gracious when I had my last stroke to take over the duties, almost as pastor, and finish the building program in the new sanctuary. He did a beautiful job of keeping the staff together and doing the many phases of work that were necessary.

I say to him all the appreciation is given in this book that

I could muster. Clayton was so faithful to take care of the duties and to see that the needs of this pastor and family were taken care of.

In 1993, Brother Mike Landry came as my co-pastor, and for one year enjoyed serving God with us. It was a real joy to work with Brother Mike. We had so much fun. It was then that he wanted to fulfill his own vision.

He resigned in good faith and was called to the pastorate of Calvary Baptist Church in Athens, Texas, with an unanimous vote. We had a big laugh, the last Wednesday night, before he left our church. He hurried home to wait for a call from Calvary Baptist Church. I was sure in my heart that they would call him, but he was not sure. He waited by the phone, and I thought, "I'll have a little fun."

I asked my son, Roger, to disguise his voice, and call Brother Mike. When the phone rang, Roger said, "Brother Mike, this is Brother Joe." He muffled his voice and said, "I'm so sorry to advise you, that you only got seventy percent of the vote, and it takes seventy-five. We don't want you to feel bad." He went on to say, "We'd still like for you to hold a revival for us."

Brother Mike said, "Well..." and stalled a minute, then he said, "Don't feel sorry about doing the will of the Lord." It was obvious that he had hit rock bottom, because all of his prayers, dreams, and visions for the church seemed to go down the drain. Toward the end of the conversation, while I was listening on the other phone, I butted in and said that we were just kidding.

Only two minutes later, a representative from Calvary did call, and told him that they had unanimously called him as their pastor. Of course, he was back on the mountain top. I thought that was funny. I don't know whether Brother Mike thought it was very funny or not, but he likes to joke, and can take a joke. We all love Brother Mike and his family.

He came to Baptist Christian Schools when he was seventeen years old. After graduating from our Academy, he then went on to Baptist Christian College and received a Masters and Doctorate Degree. He met and married Connie here and Baptist Christian held a special place in his heart.

Brother Mike was my first selection to be the man to follow me at Baptist Tabernacle. He had pastored for six years at Hope Baptist Church in Alexandria, and after two trips to the mission field in Romania, his precious son at the age of sixteen was diagnosed with severe diabetes, requiring six shots of insulin daily. This made Brother Mike unable to return to the mission field because insulin was unavailable in Romania.

Brother Mike came to preach at Baptist Tabernacle and in less than two weeks, we called him to pastor. Even though he had come for six months on furlough, he met with the men of our church and they selected him as the next pastor.

Brother Mike is my trusted friend and I have not criticized him one time. I love him dearly and he is a very godly man with convictions and one of the soundest Baptists that you will ever meet. Besides that, Brother Mike is a tremendous preacher who holds my attention. I praise him every opportunity because I have one thing I want him to know. I want to be a buddy and a friend to my pastor and with God's help I will be.

He is now forty-six years old. His three children are his oldest daughter, Amanda, who is married to our youth director, John Brinlee, Geoff, his only son, and Katie, the youngest. They are dedicated Christians for the cross and tireless workers in the church. Connie is a sweet Christian lady and is an asset to our church. I pastored her mother and father at Trinity in Doyline.

I want you to pray for Brother Mike and his family. He is known in many churches and has been used of God in Bible conferences and is a preaching machine.

May God give us many other preachers like Brother Mike Landry. People always say, "Brother Tharpe, he is just like you." I take great pride and pleasure in that because Brother Mike is a good preacher and I appreciate him more than words can ever say. Brother Mike is very mission minded and I predict great things because he is our pastor at Baptist Tabernacle.

CHAPTER 10

COMMUNE,
CHILDREN,
ILLNESS

According to the dictionary, a commune in the United States is a group of people living together, or a community. In Sibley, many years ago, the Tharpe family settled on "Tharpe Hill" in a type of commune.

Aunts, uncles, grandparents, and great-grandparents all bought or built homes close together and lived happily in this way. My grandmother lived across the street from us and my aunt lived next door, etc.

When my children first began to marry, they all lived in Shreveport, but they were scattered. For the last few years, I

have longed for them to be near me. We are a very close knit
family so it was not hard to persuade them into our current
living arrangement. Five homes make up the commune.
Corey, Roger's oldest son, is now in the process of building the
sixth with his fiancee, Jennifer. They were married in August
2003.

The vision I had, to live as I did when I was a child in
Sibley, has been almost realized. With a total of forty-nine
family members now and two on the way, it is so nice to visit
and then send them to their own homes to sleep. I call them
on the phone and ask, "What's for supper?" If I don't like what
this one is having, I call the next one. I go down the line until
I find what I am looking for.

Great food and fun are always available. These five homes
are very nice and together make a beautiful neighborhood. I
am trying to get a double-glass door installed in my house to
make sure I can watch and not miss anything that goes on in
the commune. It was wonderful and convenient when my
wife and I were sick. They were all close by to care for us. They
were only a phone call away.

We now have all our holiday meals at Kathy and Phil's
home. They built their home with the large family in mind
and a place that could contain all of us. Last year, on July 4th,
we had a big outdoor day with games such as volleyball, horse-
shoes, table games, swimming, a space walk for the little ones,
and plenty of good food and fellowship. We barbecued ham-
burgers and hot dogs with all the trimmings. We had over fifty
that day. Everyone enjoyed it so.

Thanksgiving and Christmas are also great holidays for eating the family favorite, turkey and dressing. Edith still makes the dressing for the whole bunch. All the kids agree, nobody can touch Dede's dressing.

Jonathan, our oldest grandson, started calling Edith "DeDe" when he first stated talking. She was glad because she did not want be called "Granny."

We also have a day almost every week when someone cooks the entire meal for everyone else. That way you have one day you don't have to cook, just enjoy a wonderful meal and terrific fellowship. We all look forward to that. One of my favorite sayings now is, "The commune is working!"

Kathy, because she was our firstborn, was used as a learning experience or guinea pig for how to raise children. We thought she had to be perfect. Boy, did she teach us a few lessons.

She married Phil Martin in 1969 and together they have three children, Jonathan, Rachel, and Paul, and five grandchildren. At one time, Kathy was the secretary for Dr. Collins in the college. Then she got her bachelors degree from Baptist Christian and went on to obtain her masters degree from Louisiana Tech. She worked in the mental health field for fifteen years. She was promoted to second in charge at Charter Forest Hospital and worked there for ten years. She finally suffered from burnout in that emotionally charged environment and resigned.

Her husband, Phil taught and coached for Baptist Christian Academy and College and also served as the college president. After leaving the schools, he now owns Sunbelt Multi-Residential Contractors where he works with their son, Jonathan in the construction business.

After leaving the mental health profession, Kathy and our second daughter, Sharon, decided to do something together that would be fun for them.....so they enrolled in cosmetology school and learned the nail business. They now own their own business, called 'All About Nails', where their work is play.

Their clients come for the fun of it and get their nails done at the same time. One lady said, "After being around here I've decided I want to be a member of your family. You all have such fun!" Kathy and her family live in the commune in a large two-story house and are always available to us for anything we need.

Sharon, our second born daughter, is married to Al Stephens, who is also a graduate of Baptist Christian, a teacher and a coach for many years. Together they have four children and two granddaughters. Their children are Bryan, Brandon, Heather, and Natalie. Sharon is a fun-loving person who always has a good time and wants everyone around her to enjoy her company. She worked for years as secretary to Dr. Phil Martin at the college. She has a bachelors degrees from Baptist Christian. She is a qualified teacher who doesn't like teaching. She is co-owner of All About Nails with her sister, Kathy.

Sharon lives in the "homeplace" on Gray St. where we raised all our children, but she is trying to get moved to the commune at this time. She won't be satisfied until she is out here entertaining the rest of us. She and Al do everything they possibly can to see that our needs are met. They are so kind.

Jimmy Jr., our firstborn son, also taught us some lessons about raising boys. Jim is married to Kim Green Tharpe, who is a teacher of third grade at Southern Hills Elementary School. They have a daughter, Lindsay and a son, Trey (Jimmy Gid Tharpe, III). Jim works in the car business and is currently at Westwood Auto Sales in Bossier City, Louisiana, where he has been very successful. He is a born salesman and has chosen this as his life's work. He had his own car lot at one time, but decided he didn't want that kind of responsibility. Jim also has a terrific sense of humor and exercises it all the time. He chooses to live on Cross Lake where he has a very nice two-story home. Jim loves to fish and hunt there, so he has chosen not to live with us in the commune. Jim and Kim have been so good to us in that he, along with his brothers and sisters, pay for house cleaning services weekly for us and he is always concerned about how we are doing.

Debbye, our third daughter, is a very unusual person who, according to those who know her, inherited her Dad's personality. She is married to Greg Langley and together they have six children and three grandchildren. Their children are Michelle, Jennifer, Nathan, Britany, Eric, and Melanie.

Debbye and Greg were both teachers at Southern Hills Elementary School, Debbye teaches Special Ed classes and Greg teaches Physical Education. Both of them have Masters degrees.

Early in 2002, Debbye was stricken with a very rare type of pneumonia, was hospitalized for weeks, and had extensive treatment. It has left her with permanent lung damage and she is having to use oxygen daily. On the heels of this illness, Greg had a minor knee surgery a month later, came home just fine, and was stricken with a massive stroke that same evening. Greg was a very healthy, physically fit athlete, 50 years old. He was hospitalized for months, but has made a very nice recovery. He, however, has been left disabled and not able to work either, so they have both been declared medically disabled and are no longer teaching.

They are presently trying to get well, but it has been very difficult for them as their lives were so suddenly changed and they are trying to adjust to their current situation. They live in the commune and love their home. Debbye is a wonderful soloist and has always used her voice for the Lord. Thank God for his blessings for they have also been so good to take care of us during our illnesses.

Roger, our second son, is also an unusually talented person who has been so faithful to Baptist Tabernacle. He is married to Karen Pharr Tharpe, and they have four children and one granddaughter. Their children are Gina, Corey, Dustin, and Patrick.

Roger and Karen have their own business, Bayou Contractors Services, which has been very successful. Karen worked for years as a medical assistant for a group of local dermatologists. Roger has his bachelors degree from Baptist Christian and also coached for many years. He also has a fantastic sense of humor. While coaching at Baptist Christian his team won back-to-back national championships in baseball. They have built a beautiful home in the commune. Roger and Karen have been great Christians and work tirelessly in the church. They have been so conscientious about taking good care of us and providing our care and necessities. What a comfort to have them here with us.

Brenda, our youngest daughter, has also been a blessing to our lives. She is about eight years younger than Roger and was a surprise when God gave her to us. Brenda is a single Mom, has one son, Tyler, who is now ten-years-old. Brenda has also had her share of health problems, and in the year 2000, she suffered two heart attacks. She was only 36 at the time and we surely never expected that.

Brenda has a bachelors degree from Baptist Christian and taught school for a period of time. Brenda has a terrific sense of humor and is so much fun. She lives next door to us in the commune and has helped us so many times when we were in need.

All of my children are members of Baptist Tabernacle and most of them are in regular attendance. If bad came to worse, we have a nice sized church just with my family. If you add Clayton and Linda Weaver and their children, we would have almost a hundred.

When my first five children were little, all at the same time, we were visiting one day and the lady asked me how many children we had. She said, "That's nice. How many are in school?" I told her that none of them were in school. She said, "Oh, you must have some twins." I said no to that also. We had five children in five and a half years. I was a little embarrassed for we must hold some kind of record. Another time I answered this same line of questioning. When I was asked if we were Catholic, I said, "No, just reckless Baptists."

It was not too bad when they were all little, but when they all became teenagers, then it was tough to cope with. I got to be extra busy during those years and left Edith with the job of raising them. She did a fine job, as they are really good kids and have all turned out well.

Five of my grandsons have surrendered to the ministry. They are Jonathan Martin, Nathan Lorick, Dustin Tharpe, Tyler Reid, and Greg Griffin. Nathan and his wife graduated from East Texas Baptist University in May 2003. Tyler is only 10 years old. Jonathan, Dustin, and Greg are all presently studying in the Louisiana School of Prophets.

Illness

For most of my life, I had excellent health except for tonsillitis, a bad case of mumps, and Rocky Mountain Tick Fever.

While visiting in the hospital one day, I started feeling very sick and so weak that I had to lean against the wall to keep from falling. As soon as I could I got to the doctor, and after a few tests I was diagnosed with diabetes. I did not realize at the time what a terrible disease this was nor how many problems it would cause for me in later years. I continued my bad eating habits until several things occurred. The doctor put me on pills and a diet when I refused insulin treatment. I started having neuropathy in my legs and feet, my vision began to fail, and I did not feel well much of the time.

I ignored my body's warning signs, and continued at a fast pace. I had a busy schedule pastoring Baptist Tabernacle, working in the schools, and with visions such as a mission church in Waskom, Texas, and one in Sibley, Louisiana. While trying to build a debt-free church in Sibley I found myself stressed most of the time but I did not realize what was happening to me.

One morning in March of 1992, I awoke and rose to get ready for an appointment. As I was trying to shave I noticed that my right arm was numb and not functioning properly. I awakened Edith and told her something was wrong with me. She quickly got out of bed and said, "Something has happened and we need to get you to the hospital." I knew from the beginning that it was a stroke.

My children and some of my deacons arrived at the hospital before I made it there, because on the way to the hospital I said, "Honey, please go by McDonald's and get me a sausage biscuit and a cup of coffee." I knew they would not feed me once I got to the hospital and we all know how I love to eat.

She refused and continued on to the hospital. I again insisted that she stop and she finally consented and pulled over. There was a long line at the window, so she parked the car and went inside. While inside, she looked out and saw me slumped over in the seat. She thought I was dead and came running out to see about me, but I was just resting. Clayton Weaver called on the car phone and asked where in the world we were. I asked her not to tell anyone what delayed us, but my wonderful, devoted wife told on me as soon as we got to the hospital.

Later, I was preaching in a church with Verl Gunter, a pastor in Midland, Texas. That morning the people brought sixteen sausage biscuits in two collection plates and set them on the communion table. I reached and got a biscuit and began to open it, asking them to excuse me while I ate. I have always liked to have laughter and joy and I don't believe that the sadder you look the safer you are for Heaven.

I am thankful I had no paralysis at that time, only numbness and deadness in the right arm. After the stroke I found that I would tire much easier than before. Pastoring two churches and operating six schools for years, I only had one gear and that was full speed ahead. "Retire" meant to get four new tires and keep on going.

When I was a little boy, I would run until I became weary, and then receive what my mother called my "second wind." Feeling much better, I planned to preach a message on "My Second Wind." I wanted to build the new church building, see the college and university expand, and work toward the fruition of other dreams. I so hoped to see all of my dreams come true. If not, I knew Baptist Tabernacle was on sound footing, and believed with all my heart it would keep on keeping on for God.

I was convinced that when my time was over on this earth, that God would place the right preacher at Baptist Tabernacle. I knew the only thing that would keep me out of full-time work for the Lord would be my health.

In 1998, I awoke one morning to find myself in trouble again. This time my arm and one leg were numb and my speech badly affected. I walked into the living room and my wife laughed at me. My hair was sticking up and my clothes disheveled. She said, "What's wrong with you, man? You look a sight!" Then she realized that something was definitely wrong. She quickly got me to the chair and called for help. Our neighbor, Mary Scarbro, is an EMT for the Shreveport Fire Department. She had helped us many times before. By then I was unable to speak and all I could do was make unintelligible noises. Mary told us to get to the hospital immediately.

Schumpert Hospital Emergency Room was informed that I would be coming. Members of my family and some of my church family were already gathered there when I arrived. I did not recognize any of them at the time. The next few days were very traumatic for all. I was partially paralyzed on my right side and my speech was badly affected. I was hospitalized for two months. During this process I had carotid artery surgery, and several types of therapy daily.

Edith spent night and day at the hospital for weeks. Later, when they moved me to rehab, she would go home late at night and return early the next morning. The doctors had told me of my limitations and what to expect, but often I got so discouraged I would cry myself to sleep at night after she left. My son, Jim, brought me fresh coffee every morning and prayed some of the sweetest prayers for me to get well.

God was merciful and kind and finally the wonderful day arrived and I was headed home. I called each of my children to give them the happy news. I was eager to be at home with them, and asked that they meet me there. Each of them informed me of the busy day they had, and promised to catch up with me later in the evening. Imagine my surprise when we pulled into the driveway and saw them all sitting in chairs, lined up in their birth order, outside under a huge "Welcome Home Daddy" banner.

There have since been other ailments to endure. I had two glaucoma surgeries, cataract surgery, and a cornea transplant. I no longer see well enough to read my Bible or notes when I preach. My heart is affected with eleven blockages that cannot be corrected with surgery. My right hand is partially paralyzed and I have great difficulty walking due to the neuropathy in my legs and feet.

I take many pills every day along with insulin but thank God I am still here and able to carry on. The latest ailment added to the growing list is gout, known as the "rich man's disease." My wife, who was always so healthy, had to have an emergency double by-pass surgery in 2000 and soon after, carotid artery surgery. She is doing fairly well at the moment, but no one knows what tomorrow holds. I have to depend on her so much, that she didn't get to be sick for very long.

Baptist Tabernacle was in the middle of building the new

church at the time of my second stroke, and I was disabled for so many weeks at this crucial time.   Clayton and Linda Weaver, Fletcher Caldwell, Bill Kincaid, and so many others worked tirelessly to help do their part and mine to forward the work of the Lord.   I will be forever grateful.

My sister-in-law and brother-in-law, Norma and Edd Boyd, were so faithful to me during my illness. They visited me almost every day. When I was released from the hospital, they brought me home. Even when I was in rehab, they faithfully drove me every day to my appointment. Edd has since gone home to be with the Lord and Norma has been diagnosed with cancer of the bone.

Forgiveness is one characteristic of a Christian which seems very difficult to master. One desire of mine through the years was for my people to view me as a person that forgives quickly and easily.

CHAPTER 11

50TH ANNIVERSARY
& VACATIONS

A golden wedding anniversary is an extra special event in the life of a couple. Very few live together that long in this day and time.

Edith's parents celebrated this occasion, but my parents did not since my mother died so young at 52 years of age, and my father died at 67. Our fiftieth anniversary was approaching in the year 2000, and during the year before I had been very ill from the strokes, and had discovered that I had some extreme heart blockages. It was decided that my case would not be treated by surgery because of the location of the blockages. They decided to just treat me with medications and

I still have plenty of pills to take.

When we were speaking with Dr. James Floyd, my physician, about my condition, we told him I had to hang on a little longer so that we could celebrate our 50th anniversary. He said, "When is it?" So he worked very hard at helping me to get to the anniversary. God allowed us, through the help of our doctors and medications to obtain that goal. There isn't a day that goes by that I don't thank God for Dr. Floyd.

As the time approached, all of the children, along with my nieces, Becky, Bonnie and Wanda, began to work on the gala affair. Many people helped to make it so special. They ordered invitations, mailed them, and planned the menu and decorations.

We had close to 400 to attend the magnificent event. We saw some old friends that we hadn't seen in many years. The song of the day was one made popular by Sonny and Cher, "I've Got You, Babe." I told the people how precious my wife is to me and regardless of all that may come and go, I looked at her and said, "It's okay, as long as I've got you, Babe."

We will never forget that beautiful occasion and will forever be grateful to all who worked so hard to give to us. The next day, we left for a stay in Branson, Missouri with our dear friends, the Knights and the Chelettes. Good times!!

Two years later, on our 52nd anniversary, I gave my wife the surprise of her life. I kept telling her that I had a big romantic occasion planned, and she could not know what it was. When the big day finally came, she almost begged me to tell her where we were going.

As soon as our Sunday church service was over, a big, black limousine pulled up and carried us away; not to Branson, Missouri, but where else? You guessed it. We were off to Sibley, Louisiana.

The Limousine pulled up in front of Baptist Tabernacle in Sibley and just sat there for a while. By then, she was getting irritated and told me she wanted to know what I had planned. I said, "No, you will just have to wait." By now, all the "romance" was gone and icy silence took over. About that time, Don and Louise Chelette pulled up. Things brightened up a little when she saw someone to talk to.

They got in the limousine with us and we drove down the Dorcheat Road where I told her we were going to spend the night in our camphouse. Of course, she didn't believe me or I would have been mincemeat. The limo then took us back to Sibley where we got in a car with the Chelettes.

We then had a "romantic lunch" at the Golden Biscuit, after which the car dropped us off at Calloway Corners, a very nice Bed and Breakfast. Edith was happy to discover we were not spending the night at the camphouse.

Later that afternoon, we went out and met some friends at the Golden Corral and had another nice meal. After that filling meal we drove to Baptist Tabernacle of Sibley and enjoyed a good church service. The people of the church rolled out the red carpet with a "romantic" fish fry with all the trimmings after the service. By then, Edith and I were exhausted, and quite full.

We and the Chelettes slipped away from the gathering and

that evening enjoyed the peacefulness and comfort of the Calloway Corners Bed and Breakfast. Edith had mentioned on several occasions as we passed Calloway Corners that she would enjoy staying there. I was very proud of myself, and my big surprise, but somehow I think my wife was not quite as pleased. You have to be a Tharpe by birth to love Sibley like I do.

CHAPTER 12

ONCE SAVED,
ALWAYS SAVED

Jonathan Edwards made the statement that he had three generations of his seed who all professed faith in Jesus Christ. At the same time, the noted atheist Bob Ingersol had three generations of atheists and unbelievers in his family.

I thought that my family was unusual in the fact that my grandfather was a Christian man who had two Sunday schools, one at church, and one at home. My grandfather Tharpe died when my father was eight years old.

As his boys grew up, they started drinking against their mother's wishes. The whole situation changed and Granny couldn't control their behavior. It was a hard time for the family as their positive influence of their father was over. I grew up being subjected to drinking and fighting.

After I was saved, I was instrumental in pointing many of my relatives to Christ. One of the sweetest baptismal services I ever had was when I baptized my father, mother, wife, and brothers. As I looked at the family tree that my wife had created, I realized that I had witnessed to almost everyone seeking to point him or her to faith in Christ Jesus. Today, I am the oldest living Tharpe male. I have two older female cousins, Mary Taylor and Christine Murphree.

Many have asked me why I left the Methodist faith to join the Baptist faith. First, I thank God for all my Methodist friends. A cousin, Mrs. Mattie Slater had a son, Eugene, who was a bishop in the Methodist conference in Amarillo, Texas. Word came to me that he would be happy to place me in one of the larger Methodist churches. Leon Gray, a businessman, who heard my first sermon walked out and offered to pay my tuition to Centenary College here in Shreveport. I refused this offer, but later attended Centenary at my own expense.

In Jude, the Bible speaks of special rewards for those who keep the system of faith. I surely believe that one of the cardinal doctrines from the Bible is security of the believer. The Bible is very clear on the plan of salvation and the security of the believer (Ephesians 2:8-10). Baptists have always believed in the Eighteen Articles of Faith. I believe eternal security of the believer is the greatest of these.

Many people say they believe in falling from grace, but it may be like this case. A man fell in love with a young lady whose name was Grace. They decided to elope and get married. He took a long ladder and climbed up to the second story window of Grace's bedroom.

He was unable to reach her though they had their arms outstretched to each other. With all his efforts, he could not reach her. Then the ladder broke and he fell from Grace.

The problem was that he never got to Grace. Many people are like this. They never get to Grace to start with. That is why I believe so strongly that you must be once saved. If one says he is saved, but still must have to work, salvation is not a gift through grace, but by works.

I have always believed that salvation is by grace through faith, not of works. And that is why I am now a Baptist, by conviction and an Independent Baptist by eviction. Independent Baptists go all the way back to John's baptism on the sunny shores of Galilee. There are only two schools of thought...works or grace. This is why I am an Independent Baptist.

Almost all religions believe in works for salvation, except Baptists, and a handful of those who do not call themselves Baptists. My mother, before she became a Baptist, while discussing this said, "Jimmy, I'm not going to do anything bad enough to lose my salvation." She was depending on her good works. After she became a Baptist, she understood this doctrine. Ephesians 2:9, "Lest any man should boast." No man will ever get to heaven and boast that he got there without accepting Christ. That is why Jesus shed his blood so that every man could be saved.

I am so happy to say that I have many Methodist friends

who are saved. There are only three ways that a person can have fellowship.

In Adam, all are brothers and sisters

In Christ, all are my brothers and sisters, regardless of denomination

In Doctrine, the Bible speaks of a system of faith in the book of Jude. It tells us to earnestly contend for the faith once delivered to the saints.

I believe there will be special rewards in heaven for those people who have kept the system of faith. I am a member of a church that teaches the faith once delivered to the saints. You need to be in a church that teaches this system.

The following is a condensed sermon that I have preached several times, "Once Saved, Always Saved." I have always believed that God does the saving and the keeping of the believer in order for a man to enter heaven. I make no differences in the plan of salvation and the security, Romans 11:6. There is no mixture. Either a man is saved by works or saved by faith.

I grew up as a Methodist and didn't go to church but a very few times. I didn't know anything at all about the plan of Salvation until I was almost 20 years old. I had never heard the true plan of redemption or the statement, "you must be born again." That may sound strange to some of you who were saved early and grew up in a Christian home. Perhaps some of you may have a testimony similar to mine and you too can thank God for the blood of Jesus Christ.

After I was saved, God called me to preach and after surrendering to His call, I was a Methodist preacher for about six months. I was offered four charges (churches) in the Methodist group.

One day, by means of the sweet Holy Spirit, God spoke to me and I began to study a "Baptist Way" book. This book is about the way Baptists believe, and I thank God that through prayer and the leadership of the Holy Spirit, I found what I believed to be the closest to the New Testament church.

I joined Calvary Baptist Church in Minden, Louisiana, followed the Lord in baptism and became a member of a New Testament Baptist Church. Since that time, the doctrine of the "security of the saved" means more to me than most other doctrines because this is the one that caused me to become a Baptist.

We are living in a day when God's people need to hear doctrine. I meet Baptists almost every week that do not believe in "once saved, always saved." I also know Baptists who could not quote two scriptures to show that one is eternally saved, even if their lives depended upon it. I believe God wants us to be better skilled in His Word.

"Security of the believer" is a beautiful doctrine and can be brought to light if we take God's Word and just believe it. Some may say they believe in "falling from grace," but you can't show me one clear-cut scripture that indicates this false belief. God's Word just does not teach this.

I am not as concerned about whether you're going to lose

your salvation as I am about whether you were really saved to start with. That's the problem with most folks today...they've never been saved! I truly believe that many Baptists are lost and on the road to hell because they failed to get saved. Now, I want us to consider, "once saved."

I. ONCE SAVED

I want to ask you some personal questions to begin with. Are you really saved? Do you know the Lord Jesus Christ as your Savior? Is there a time in your life when you were "once saved?"

So many people answer by saying, "Preacher, I just don't remember." Well, who would remember it, if you don't? You don't have to remember the exact day or hour, but you'd better remember that there was a time when the new birth presented a change in you. We read in II Corinthians 5:17, "Therefore if any man be in Christ, he is a new creature: old things are passed away; behold, all things are become new."

"I'm tired of folks who say they're saved and then live like the Devil." They don't come to the House of God, act as if they hate Gospel music, seldom read His Word, never witness to anybody and seldom pray. A saved person becomes a new creature. You cannot be born again and become a new creature without knowing when it happened!

In John 3:3, we read, "...except a man be born again, he cannot see the kingdom of God." In verse 7 of that same chapter, we read, "...ye must be born again." It doesn't say that it would be a good thing to be born again, nor is it a recommendation that you be born again. The Bible teaches that you **must** be born again.

Ephesians 2:8-9 states, "By grace are ye saved, through faith; and that not of yourselves: it is the gift of God. Not of works lest any man should boast." The plan of redemption is made plain here. You can't boast of being saved, except through the blood of Christ. No one will ever stand before the throne of God and say, "I'm here because I lived a good life," or, "I'm here because I was able to stand on my own merits to gain heaven." You'll only get to Heaven because Jesus Christ saved you and He has the power to keep you.

All people fit under one of two religions - one of works and the other of faith. All churches and preachers that teach and preach falling from grace depend on what they do to get to heaven, and not what God has done for them.

The way of salvation is "by grace...through faith...not of yourselves: it is the gift of God." You can't work for it! It is something God gives you in the form of faith and that's what makes it so precious and sweet. We read in Titus 3:5, "Not by the works of righteousness which we have done, but according to his mercy he saved us..."

In John 4:10, Jesus told the woman at the well, "If thou knewest the gift of God, and who it is that saith to thee, Give me to drink; thou wouldest have asked of him, and he would have given thee living water." Salvation is a gift and you don't have to work for it in order to keep it. If it's the way you live after you're saved that determines whether you keep it or lose it, then it's not God's grace that saved you...it's your good works. The Bible tells us again in Romans 6:23, "...the wages of sin is death, but the gift of God is eternal life."

It is possible for a lost person to be a good person, even be a church member and not be saved. "Once saved" means there was a time and place in your life when you really got saved. A rich ruler ran to Christ, kneeled down, and asked how to inherit eternal life. Jesus looked into the face of a good man who had kept much of the law, but he was on the road to hell.

The thief on the cross had lived a rotten life, and even while nailed to the wood was saved in the last moment because he rejected his righteousness and accepted the right-eousness of Christ. Nicodemus was a ruler of the Jews, a mem-ber of the Sanhedrin court, a good person and a man who believed in good living...yet he was lost and on the road to Hell. Jesus said, "...ye must be born again"(John 3).

We read in the word of God of the Pharisees who dogged the steps of Jesus Christ. Pharisees were self-righteous, reli-gious people, but lost. They gave their money, prayed, and wanted to be seen of men. Jesus indicated one day when he pointed to a street-walking woman, "that harlot will get to Heaven before you will."

We read about Cornelius in the Bible of how he prayed, was sincere, gave his money and was known to be a man who had a good name...yet, Peter had to go and show him words whereby he could be saved.

You see it's one thing to be a "good person" and another thing to be a "saved person." There are many good people, but good for nothing. Unless we get born again, (saved, regenerated), with a new life and have a time and place when we were "once saved," we will not make Heaven! There is a song that goes, "...without Jesus, you won't make Heaven." Are you "once saved?"

If you are deceived on this one thing, you'll miss Heaven. I'd rather be wrong on a thousand things and be right on the new birth and make it to Heaven. We must face ourselves in the sight of God.

When Jesus saves us, He lives within and we are partakers of His Divine nature. This is the part that thousands have never experienced. You must be "once saved" and when you get that part settled, you'll have the "always saved" bit settled.

I see people get saved in our church all the time that are already church members and have been for years. I've seen missionaries, preachers, deacons, and Sunday School Superintendents saved. It is possible for preachers to preach and then later really get saved. There had to be a time when they rejoiced in Jesus Christ as their Savior when they were "once saved."

People need to go to the Bible, then thank God for what they are doctrinally. Somebody said that Adam fell from grace, but Adam didn't know one thing about grace until the animals were killed and blood was shed in the Garden. Then, he and Eve were born again. You see, he stood on his own merits and knew nothing of grace until he was saved. After he sinned, he had to get saved (born again, blood-washed)...just like you and me.

We read about Judas (one of the twelve) who some say,

"Fell from grace." The Bible indicates in John 6:70-71, "Judas was a devil from the beginning." He was never saved. Someone said the angels were cast out of Heaven and fell from grace, but the Bible teaches that an angel has never been born again. They too, stand on their own merits.

One thing I am sure of is that I am saved. Someone asked, "preacher, don't you believe that you can backslide?" The answer to that is yes! Every saved person knows what backsliding is because they've experienced it. There are no perfect people anywhere!

II. ALWAYS SAVED

We read in I Corinthians 5:1-5, "It is reported that there is fornication among you, and such fornication as is not so much named among the Gentiles, that one should have his father's wife. And ye are puffed up, and have not rather mourned; that he that hath done this deed might be taken away from among you. For I verily, as absent in body, but present in spirit, have judged already, as though I were present, concerning him that hath so done this deed, In the name of our Lord Jesus Christ, when ye are gathered together, and my spirit, with the power of our Lord Jesus Christ, To deliver such and one unto Satan for the destruction of the flesh that the spirit may be saved in the day of the Lord Jesus."

In this passage, we are told of a man who ran off with his father's wife (no doubt, his step-mother). Paul said the man ought to be turned over to the devil for the destruction of the flesh so that his spirit might be saved in the last day. If you will not serve God (after you're saved), sometimes He turns you over to the devil. I believe this is why we have some premature deaths of Christian people.

If you become a disobedient child, the rod of correction is waiting for you. In I Corinthians 3:11-15 we read, "For other foundation can no man lay than that is laid, which is Jesus Christ. Now if any man build upon this foundation gold, silver, precious stone, wood, hay, stubble; Every man's work shall be made manifest: for the day shall declare it, because it shall be revealed by fire; and the fire shall try every man's work of what sort it is. If any man's work abides which he hath built thereupon, he shall receive a reward. If any man's work shall be burned, he shall suffer loss: but he himself shall be saved; yet so as by fire."

Some will stand before God and see their works burn even though they will be saved, yet as by fire. These are they who refused to put God first in their lives. It's one thing to be saved and not have your life on God's altar in service and sacrifice. These are things we must see!

"Once saved, always saved" will give all the glory to Jesus Christ. Preachers who preach falling from grace are saying salvation is based on works. You will be disappointed if you're depending on salvation by works, because you're depending on the mercy of the devil instead of the grace of God. The belief in salvation by works also gives Satan more power than God, and God has never given Satan more power than He, Himself has.

This would also reflect on the blood of Jesus Christ. Jesus

does the saving and the keeping. In John 3:16 we read "For God so loved the world that He gave His only begotten son, that whosoever believeth in Him should not perish but have everlasting life."

I want to back up by saying, "amen, you should not perish!" You can take John 3:16 and prove the eternal security of the saved and you won't have to go anywhere else, but let us go on further and read John 5:24, "...He that heareth my word, and believeth on him that sent me, hath everlasting life, and shall not come into condemnation; but is passed from death unto life."

That's why Jesus said, "if you'll believe in me, you'll never die." Why? Because you've already passed from death unto life and you can't pass back from life into death.

In John 3:36 we read, "He that hath the Son hath life. He that hath not the son, hath not life, but the wrath of God abideth on Him."

The great Apostle Paul said. "I know whom I have believed and I'm persuaded He's able to keep that which I've committed unto Him against that day" (II Timothy 1:12).

Jesus prayed, "Holy Father, keep through thine own name those whom thou hast given me." (John 17:11) The Bible teaches in John 10:27, "My sheep hear my voice and I know them, and they follow me. And I give unto them eternal life and they shall never perish; neither shall any man pluck them out of my hand. My Father, which gave them me, is greater than all; and no man is able to pluck them out of my Father's hand."

In Jude 24 we read, "Now unto him that is able to keep you from falling, and to present you faultless before the presence of his glory with exceeding joy."

Jesus said, "I am the bread of life, he that cometh to me shall never hunger..." (John 6:35). In John 4:13, Jesus said to the woman at the well, "Whosoever drinketh of this water shall thirst again, But whosoever drinketh of the water that I shall give him shall never thirst, but the water that I shall give him shall be in him a well of water springing up into everlasting life." All that the Father giveth me shall come to me; and him that cometh to me I will in no wise cast out" (John 6:37).

In Psalm 37:23-28, we find that "The steps of a good man are ordered by the Lord: and he delighteth in his way. Though he fall, he shall not be utterly cast down: for the Lord upholdeth him with his hand, I have been young, and now am old; yet have I not seen the righteous forsaken, nor his seed begging bread." The Bible said his seed is preserved forever!

The question is asked in Romans 8:35, who shall separate us from the love of Christ?" Please read this passage of Scripture and see how powerful it really is. Paul said, "I am persuaded that neither death..." or any of these things mentioned can get my salvation.

Samson, who died with his enemies, could testify to this. Though he took his own life, he died in Jesus Christ. Moses and others God killed and took home prematurely will meet us in Heaven.

You may ask, "Preacher, what happens if a saved person sins and gets out of the will of God?" Read Hebrews 12:5 and find the answer. In verse 8 of that chapter we read, "If you be without chastisement, whereof all are partakers, then ye are bastards, and not sons."

When a child of God sins, the chastisement of God will come. We read in Hebrews 12:9, "Furthermore we have had fathers of flesh which corrected us, and we gave them reverence..." You'd better believe this and thank God for it. "Shall we not much rather be in subjection unto the Father of spirits, and live?" Some never see the words, "and live.."

I believe when you fail to do God's will and take the attitude, "I'll do what I please"... then you are subject to chastisement. You may say, "I don't care what the preacher preaches, I'll go on and drink liquor, I'll withhold my tithes, I refuse to read my Bible, nor do I have to attend Sunday's services!"

With this attitude, you'd better be careful, because you're one of the best prospects to die early. When you rebel against God, He knows how to deal with you. God is a loving God, but He is also a God of wrath with a rod of correction.

There is no such thing as "hard luck." Every blade of grass has a purpose and God Almighty knows every heartbeat and even the numbers of the hairs on your head. When we get out of line, we pay for it. It may be a trip to the cemetery to bury a loved one, or we may even be flat on our back due to illness, but God will whip a Christian!

When Samson (who was a man of God) sinned, he lost his eyes, his respect and finally lost his life. He didn't lose his salvation. He lost his joy, then his life. God's Word teaches that Moses died a premature death because he smote the rock instead of speaking to it. He died because of disobedience to God.

David sinned by committing adultery, then tried to hide it by murder. God did not take his salvation, but he did take his joy. David said in Psalm 51:12, "restore unto me the joy of thy salvation." Losing your joy is probably the worst of all chastisements. Yes, God chastens His children.

When a person is born again, he can never become unborn. There is no place in God's Word where one is born the third time. The new birth is a one-time experience and if this were not true, then you would lose your salvation and have to be born the third time.

The story is told of a little boy who was playing with a friend and during their play, he hit her on purpose. The boy's mother said, "Johnny, if you don't behave yourself, I'll whip you!" It happened again and Johnny got his whipping. Then, in a few minutes, he struck his friend again.

This time the mother took Johnny by the hand and said, "I'm taking you home because you will not behave." When God's children are disobedient and will not mind Him, sometimes He takes us by the hand and takes us home to Glory.

My friend, please trust Jesus Christ as your precious Savior today. Let Heaven come down and fill your soul. We read in John 6:37, "All that the Father giveth me shall come to me and him that cometh to me, I will in no wise cast out." Jesus said in Romans 10:13, "Whosoever shall call upon the name of the Lord shall be saved."

Ask Him now and He will give you eternal life.

Pastors, always remember there are two kinds of people in this world, the realists and the dreamers. The realists know where they're going. The dreamers have already been there.

CHAPTER 13

THE GREATNESS OF THE CHURCH OF JESUS CHRIST

"And I say unto thee, That thou art Peter, and upon this rock I will build my church; and the gates of hell shall not prevail against it" (Matthew 16:18).

I do not know of any subject dearer to my heart than the church. I believe that if one loves Christ, that person will also love the church of the living God. The church is the greatest public institution in existence. The church is divine in its origin, in its ordinances, and in its objectives. The church is more than a brotherhood organization, more than an educational institution, and more than a governmental institution.

We read in Ephesians 2:20, "And are built upon the foundation of the apostles and prophets, Jesus Christ himself being the Chief Cornerstone." When God got ready to build His Church He used the material that John the Baptist had prepared. These born-again believers who had been baptized at the hand of John, who was commissioned from heaven, made up the church of our Lord. The founder, Jesus Himself, became the Chief Cornerstone. This is wonderful to think about. Let us consider the greatness of this church.

I. THE GREATNESS OF THE CHURCH OF CHRIST IS FOUND IN THE GREATNESS OF ITS HISTORY.

When we study history we learn that many great institutions have been built and have fallen to the dust of the earth. But I am grateful that we have a record in the Word of God of an institution that shall never fall nor fail. It has a historical record that reaches back to the sunny shores of Galilee.

> "And Jesus, walking by the sea of Galilee, saw two brethren, Simon called Peter, and Andrew his brother, casting a net into the sea; for they were fishers. And he saith unto them, Follow me, and I will make you fishers of men" (Matthew 4:18,19).

That institution is the church that Jesus built. Its history and the trail of blood left behind it will stand today and testify to the greatness of Almighty God.

When Jesus stood one day and said, "Upon this rock I will build my church," He distinguished it from all others; a kind of church that will preach and teach the truth to all nations. The gates of Hell shall not prevail against it. It is founded on the greatness of Jesus Christ.

It was my sweet privilege to stand on the shores of Galilee near where, I suppose, Jesus called out the first four disciples. It was here that the church began the greatest institution on earth, which will live on until Jesus comes again. It is a wonderful privilege to be a part of the New Testament Church. It is a great thing to know that we have a church with a doctrine that goes back in history to the Lord Himself, and that we are not following some man or some idea.

II. THE GREATNESS OF THE CHURCH OF CHRIST IS FOUND IN ITS PURPOSE

The primary purpose of the church is to preach the gospel that souls may be saved.

"The thief cometh not, but for to steal, and to kill, and to destroy: I am come that they might have life, and they might have it more abundantly" (John 10:10).

"For what is a man profited if he shall gain the whole world, and lose his own soul? Or what shall a man give in exchange for his soul" (Matthew 16:26)?

In Matthew 4:23 we read, "And Jesus went about all
Galilee, teaching in their synagogues, and preaching the
gospel of the kingdom, and healing all manner of disease
among the people." If we miss the purpose of the Gospel, we
have missed everything. What is the purpose of our gather-
ings? "To reach the lost." What is the purpose of our Sunday
schools? "To reach the lost." The purpose of the church is to
utilize the whole man – the mind, body, and soul. Its purpose
is expressed in the ministry of Jesus Christ. Jesus was concerned with saving souls. He loved and taught people. He
taught their minds, saved their souls, and healed their bodies.
He left a work for the church to carry on which is to preach
the gospel and minister to the sick and needs. When we minister in this manner, we are pleasing God.

III. THE GREATNESS OF THE CHURCH OF CHRIST IS FOUND IN ITS SUPREME TASK

What is the supreme task? It is to proclaim the gospel to
all people.

"Go ye therefore, and teach all nations, baptizing them
in the name of the Father, and of the Son, and of the
Holy Ghost: teaching them to observe all things whatsoever I have commanded you: and, lo, I am with you
alway, even unto the end of the world" (Matthew
28:19.20).

The task is not only to win the lost, but to train the converts after they have come to Christ. Under this Great Commission we find the marching orders for the church.

> "For I delivered unto you first of all that which I also received, how that Christ died for our sins according to the scriptures" (I Corinthians. 15:3).

> "This is a faithful saying, and worthy of all acceptation, that Christ Jesus came into the world to save sinners of whom I am chief" (I Timothy. 1:15).

Some churches are only interested in the physical aspects of buildings, and other material things. The Bible teaches that we should be interested in souls and spiritual values and in turning backsliders back to God. We need to have lost people on our hearts, and a prayer to God to reach their eternity-bound souls before it is too late.

> "Go ye into all the world, and preach the gospel to every creature" (Mark 16:15).

> "But ye shall receive power, after that the Holy Ghost is come upon you: and ye shall be witnesses unto me both in Jerusalem, and in all Judea, and in Samaria, and unto the uttermost part of the earth" (Acts 1:8).

The task demands that the church take a firm stand against all sin. Too many people, including preachers, are taking sin lightly.

> "I beseech you therefore, brethren, by the mercies of
> God, that ye present your bodies a living sacrifice,
> holy, acceptable, unto God, which is your reasonable
> service" (Romans 12:1).

The church must be in the world, but not of the world.

Members of the Shreveport, LA., Baptist Tabernacle are urged to live clean, separated, dedicated, spirit-filled lives and show the world that there is greatness in the New Testament Church. Among other things, our members are urged not to go to movies, nor dress immodestly, nor drink alcoholic beverages, nor use tobacco in any form. Mr. And Mrs. Tegarden were Southern Baptists who visited our church for three services. They did not see any smoking on the church grounds. Their conviction as Baptist and their firm stand against the use of tobacco caused them to consider the Baptist Tabernacle as their church home. Shortly after they were received into our church, they deeded their four two-story rental apartments and furnishings, their home and property, with an appraised value of $50,000.00 to the church. God has great things for a church that will dare to be different and preach the whole council of God. The task of the church is great and every member will answer for any failure of the church. When a person criticizes the church of which he is a member, he criticizes himself, for he is a part of the church. God is proud of the church member who will fall in and go to work, one who will find the weak places and strengthen them. It is the duty of a church member to share his part of the responsibility and load. A good church member should be regular in attendance, a tither, and a soul winner. Brag on you church as being the greatest church in all the world. Why? Because Jesus bought it with His blood. Christ loved His church and gave Himself for it. Do your part to help present the church as a bride without spot or blemish.

IV. THE GREATNESS OF THE CHURCH OF CHRIST IS FOUND IN THE GREATNESS OF ITS PEOPLE

Do you know what makes a church great? It isn't the church building, even though buildings cannot be minimized. Baptized believers, who have covenanted together to carry out the commands of the Lord, make His church great.

The church is the institutional embodiment of the principles of the Kingdom of God. Yes, people who pray and live powerful lives under the influence of the Holy Spirit make the church great. These people are not only church workers but soul winners who are after the lost for Christ.

"They that sow in tears shall reap in joy. He that goeth forth and weepeth, bearing precious seed, shall doubtless come again with rejoicing, bringing his sheaves with him" (Psalm 126:5,6).

The greatness of the church is not in its geographical location, the number of its members, the amount of its wealth, but its greatness is found in the character of the people who compose its body.

When we let our standard of living fall to a low level, we are a disgrace to God. We fail to show the world the radiance of the Spirit in our hearts. God help us to see that the greatness of the church will be seen in the lives of her people.

> "Ye are the salt of the earth; but if the salt have lost its savour, wherewith shall it be salted? It is thenceforth good for nothing, but to be cast out, and to be trodden under the foot of men" (Matthew. 5:13).

V. THE GREATNESS OF THE CHURCH OF CHRIST IS FOUND IN THE GREATNESS OF ITS FOUNDER

If I were not a member of a church with doctrines, like the one Christ founded, holding forth the precious doctrines He preached, I would be diligently searching for what I believed to be the truth.

> "And are built upon the foundation of the apostles and prophets, Jesus Christ himself being the chief cornerstone" (Ephesians. 2:20).

> "And hath put all things under his feet, and gave him to be the head over all things to the church, which is his body, the fulness of him that filleth all in all" (Ephesians. 1:22,23).

Christ is great in every way; in His nature, in His power,

in His character, and in His Eternal Purpose.

When we accept Christ, join His church, and are scripturally baptized, we accept the greatest challenge in the world. Some of our Baptists are busy today preaching that we should teach all things. We should; I would not minimize that. But I tell you that the greatness of the church is found in the first part of that Great Commission, "Go ye therefore into all the world." Before people can be baptized they must be saved. Before they are saved we must go after them. That's the greatness of the church and the Founder set it up this way. He sent His followers out in groups of two to witness. If we love Jesus, we will love His church and be willing to witness for Him. We will be willing to live for Him or even to die for Him, if it were necessary, Many martyrs have died in the past for the sake of Christ and I thank God that what they represented could not be killed. How wonderful to know that His church, which cradles the truth, lives on today. I'm so grateful that I have a part in it, and in the program of God that has an answer to every problem in America, yea even in the whole world.

Our Saviour did not organize a big, universal, mystical body. He organized a local church with a group of baptized believers who covenanted together in an assembly to carry out His commands. It is a privilege to be a part of it. Great blessings are in store for those who keep the doors of the church open. People who will put Christ first, who will dare to be different, who will suffer for His cause, are the ones who believe that His church is great. Those who only come to church when they get ready, and have little concern for the welfare of the church, are they who do not believe that the church is great. The Bible says that Christ loved His church and gave Himself for it. "Husbands, love your wives, even as Christ loved the church, and gave himself for it" (Ephesians. 5:25).

It is great in the eyes of God and it can be great to you if you will think seriously about it. When you support it with your talents, time, and tithes, it becomes dear to your heart. As you put more and more of yourself into the church it becomes greater to you. Every member should help push it forward so that the world can see Jesus and the radiance of His wonderful love.

Many today should repent and say, "Oh, God, I haven't done right toward you and your church. I'm a Christian, but I haven't seen the greatness of the church as I should. I've let God down, and I'm going to renew my vows to the church that Jesus loved and gave Himself for."

A New Testament church is the bulwark of the truth. It is the only thing God ever set up that He promised to be with us to the end, and even said the gates of Hell should not prevail against it. It is the only institution Jesus said He would get glory in. "Unto him be glory in the church by Christ Jesus throughout all ages, world without end."

His glory is not in mass evangelism, but in His church. You can help make it great by being a factor in it and a power for it.

You, who are lost without Jesus, should receive Him unto your heart and life. If you will repent of your sins, trust Him, and put Him first, you will experience the sweetest joy in all the world. After you are saved, offer yourself for scriptural baptism in a New Testament church and serve Him faithfully. You will receive the "peace that passeth all understanding."

Some people have dynamite gospel, but live a firecracker life. One should live a spiritual life mindful of the blessings of God.

CHAPTER 14

GREAT MONUMENTS OF THE NEW TESTAMENT CHURCH

"And he took bread, and gave thanks, and brake it, and gave unto them, saying, This is my body, which is given for you; this do in remembrance of me" (Luke 22:19).

"And he said, Go into the city to such a man, and say unto him, The Master saith, My time is at hand; I will keep the Passover at thy house with my disciples" (Matthew 26:18).

"After the same manner also he took the cup, when he had supped, saying, This cup is the new testament in my blood: this do ye, as oft as ye drink it, in remembrance of me" (I Corinthians 11:25).

"Know ye not, that so many of us as were baptized into Jesus Christ were baptized into his death? Therefore we are buried with him by baptism into death; that like as Christ was raised up from the dead by the glory of the Father, even so we also should walk in newness of life" (Romans 6:3-4).

Much of the Old Testament worship was by types and shadows of things to come. It was a worship of faith in future events. In all ages, people have been saved by personal faith in Christ, the Saviour. Before Christ came, souls were saved by faith in Christ's coming. To assist in coming to such faith, God gave the old Jews certain forms of worship that pointed to the coming Messiah; namely, the Priest, who was the go-between for God and man, which points to Christ and His cross as The Great High Priest forever, after the order of Melchisedec. Also, the uplifted serpent in the wilderness pointed to the uplifted Christ on the cross who cures all the poison of sin in the soul of the believer. Again, the scapegoat was typical of Christ who bore our sins away and died upon the cross for us.

The sacrifice and atonement pointed directly to Christ crucified. We will remember that once each year, the Jewish people killed a lamb in the outer court of the Temple and burned its body as a sacrifice, but the high priest took the blood of the lamb and went back to the veil of the temple into the Holy Place and there, on the mercy seat, sprinkled the blood as an atonement for the sins of the people. This sacrifice and atonement were shadows of the Lamb of God who the people killed without the courts of heaven by crucifixion, which was the "Supreme Sacrifice." The sacrifice made it possible for all who would repent and believe to be saved. All may be saved if they believe. That is what Christ's death on the cross did for all men. *"Whosoever will may come."* Then Christ, the Great High Priest, took His own blood into the Holy of Holies of Heaven and there, on the mercy seat, made atonement for all believers.

Therefore, we can readily see that much of the Old Testament pointed to Christ or revealed some blessed work that Christ was to do for sinners. Now, since Christ came, the types and shadows of the Old Testament are not needed. If we have our mothers with us, we do not need a picture to remind us of them. Christ has already come and done away with the Old Testament forms of worship; the types and shadows that were to remind the people of the coming Messiah.

Since Christ's suffering on the cross was the supreme act of redemption, we are to forever keep vividly before us this "Supreme Sacrifice." Therefore, Jesus put this side of the cross, and in His church, two ordinances which are to point us back to the cross where Christ died, *"the just for the unjust, that He might bring us to God,"* just as the Old testament types and shadows pointed up to Christ and the Cross. These church ordinances are memorial services to be kept within the church, for the church and to be administered by the church. They are monuments of Christ's broken body and shed blood also of his death, burial and resurrection. Monuments in the Bible were memorials of men's deeds, but the monuments within the New Testament Church are exclusively for the cross of Christ, with its suffering, death, burial and resurrection.

There are many monuments in the Bible. For example, a monument was erected by Jacob and Laban. This memorial was to commemorate a covenant between them and was sworn to, that neither would pass the monument to do the other harm. They sealed this agreement with the words, *"The Lord watch between me and thee while we are absent one from another."* Again, Joshua and the children of Israel set up twelve stones as a monument to God for leading them safely across the swollen Jordan River. This monument was forever to keep vividly in the minds of the coming Jewish generations that God had safely led His people across the Jordan into the promised land. Samuel erected a monument to commemorate a great victory over the Philistines. Samuel called the place where the monument was erected *"Ebenezer,"* saying *"Hither to hath the Lord helped us."*

The Passover Feast was a memorial to commemorate the passing of the death angel over the Jewish families when blood had been sprinkled over the doors and on the door posts of each Jewish home. Today, the Jews still observe the Passover, which points them back to the passing over of the death angel in the land of Egypt.

There are also a few monuments in the New Testament. For example, Mary anointed Jesus with the precious ointment. Jesus said of her, *"wheresoever this Gospel shall be preached throughout the whole world, this also that she hath done shall be spoken of for a memorial of her."*

Now we come to the two memorials Jesus placed in the New Testament Church. As a whole, memorials were erected to the living deeds of men. For example, there is a statue of General Lee at Gettysburg which represents him in his fullest power, as a military genius. But the monuments which Christ erected to Himself were not to His life, as wonderful as that was. Neither of these monuments point to His virgin birth, nor to His matchless, sinless life, nor His deeds of doing good or showing kindness, nor His incomparable teachings; but these monuments are for the purpose of commemorating Christ's death. It is true we commemorate His birth and resurrection, but not according to His instructions. Some even observe Good Friday, commemorating His suffering, but Jesus placed the commemoration of His death as an ordinance in His local church. The church is a group of scripturally baptized believers who have covenanted together to carry out the commands of our Lord. The church is the institutional embodiment of the principles of the Kingdom of God.

Monuments to illustrious persons are held sacred. For example, the monument to our heroes carved in the Black Hills of South Dakota, the monument on Grant Mountain in Atlanta, Ga., and Washington's Tomb in Mount Vernon are held sacred. To deface one of them would bring condemnation from every true American. When a monument is defaced by some vandal, we demand that such vandal be apprehended and severely punished. In Kansas City a statue of the Indian Scout stood in Penn Park and some vandal broke certain parts of the statue off and carried them away. Tempers ran high and blood boiled in the veins of most of the people in Kansas City. There was a loud outcry that the culprit should be apprehended and punished. However, we have stood by and watched vandals defacing the monuments that Jesus put in His local church, that are to point us back to His broken body, shed blood, and to His death, burial and resurrection, and we have said little about it. It is wrong to take alien immersion and to open the Lord's Supper to all Christians or all denominations. This turns the ordinance into a love feast. Only a sound local Baptist church has the authority to administer Baptism and the Lord's Supper.

These vandals have been defacing the first monument that Christ erected to point us back to His broken body and shed blood. We have had certain groups chipping away at this beautiful monument for centuries, by teaching what is known as transubstantiation. That is, that the unleavened bread and fruit of the vine have been changed into the actual blood and flesh of Christ's human body. They believe in the Lord's Supper, but it must be called the Eucharist and it must have saving power. This same group has chipped away further at Christ's monument by teaching that the laity are to partake only of the bread, while the priest drinks the wine. But Jesus said to His infant church, while speaking of the cup, *"Take ye*

and drink ye all of it, for this is my blood of the New Testament."
Jesus knew that this group would deface His monument, so
He distinctly informed us that the entire church was to partake of the emblems representing His broken body and shed
blood. The two ordinances are restricted to the local church
where one holds his or her membership.

Then, we have other vandals defacing this monument who
teach what is known as con-substantiation. That is, that
Christ's body and blood are present with the bread and fruit
of the vine. Not that it is Christ's real flesh and blood, but that
Christ's flesh and blood are present in the emblems.

There are still other vandals that teach that this monument is to celebrate Christian love. Therefore, some of them
observe love feasts. Some of our protestant denominations
have gone so far along this line as to have union services in
some public hall or auditorium and all who wish to partake of
the supper are invited to do so. They have forgotten that the
ordinance was placed within the church and for the church,
and to be administered by the church. Still others are defacing
this monument by carrying the emblems to some on the bat-
tlefield and into homes and hospitals and administering to
shut-ins and ill people. There are many other vandals that are
defacing this monument but space will not permit me here to
name them.

Now let us look at the second monument which Christ
placed in His New Testament Church, which is the ordinance
of baptism. It is to point us back to Christ's death, burial and
resurrection. It is also a public declaration that the one being

baptized has died to the old life of service to Satan and sin, and therefore, they are buried to that old life in the baptismal waters, showing that they are dead to their past and, since they are dead, they are buried in the beautiful waters of baptism. Then they are brought up out of the water as a picture of their resurrection from their death in sin, to walk in the resurrection or newness of life. Baptism is salvation pictured in water colors.

The ordinance also points us to the final death of our physical bodies and to our burial in the City of the Dead and the beautiful resurrection. However, the primary purpose of this ordinance is to commemorate the death, burial and resurrection of Jesus. Many vandals have also been chipping at the monument of Baptism through the centuries.

The first defacement of the monument of Baptism was about the year of A.D. 250. It happened in this way. Novation, an old Roman Emperor, was as he thought, on his death bed. He had come to believe there was something in Christianity and that the benefit would be derived at the hour of baptism, therefore, he requested baptism. Since he was so ill that he could not be immersed, they brought water and poured it upon him and around him, to resemble as nearly as possible, immersion. A report of this case may be found in Dr. Chase's *Design of Baptism*, page 53, also Bingham's *Christian Antiquity*, chapter 11, section 14, and Dr. Wall's *History of Infant Baptism*, part 2, chapter 9, page 463, and especially one of the Early Church Fathers, *Eusebius's Ecclesiastical History*, Book 6, page 43. This is the first incident of chipping at this monument to be found by the best historians that we have ever had.

Immersion was practiced so generally that when Constantine conquered the Gauls, he gave them their choice of baptism or the sword. Most of them chose baptism and Constantine's soldiers took the soldiers of Gaul into the Danube River and immersed them. The early churches had baptisteries built within them. There were many public baptismal founts. Some of those are preserved until this day.

The Edinburg Encyclopedia says, "The first law to sanction Aspersion as a mode of baptism, was Pope Stevens II, A.D. 753, but it was not until 1311 that a council at Ravenna declared immersion or sprinkling to be indifferent. In Scotland, however, sprinkling was never practiced in ordinary cases until the reign of Edward IV in about 1550, for immersion was commonly observed."

With the baptism of Novation, the heresy of regenerational baptism developed. Therefore, it was thought necessary that infants be baptized or be lost. Infants cannot very well be immersed, therefore, the fallacy of sprinkling babies began to be practiced. This is one of the most hurtful heresies that has ever crept into the Christian religion. A baby cannot be brought to the Lord's Supper. How could these ordinances point the baby back to the broken body, shed blood, death, burial, and resurrection of Christ before the Child reaches the age of accountability? This fateful heresy is in conflict with the atonement of Christ. It lays stress upon water to wash the soul white and not upon the shed blood of Jesus. Can you imagine a baby in glory singing, unto him who sprinkled water on me and washed me clean and not unto him who washed me in

His own blood?

Also, sprinkling of infants has introduced into the visible church, a non-regenerated membership, for these churches largely consider that the baby has been introduced into the church. This blots out all lines of distinction between the regenerated church member and the unregenerated world. In some cases, those who believe this fallacy do not claim that the christening of the baby renews its moral nature so as to make it a saint, but they do claim it introduced the child into the church. Infant baptism has two terrible evils about it. The first is the harm that it does to the church. It fills the church with unregenerated people. The most corrupt churches on earth are those of Europe which are filled up with those who were sprinkled in infancy and never led to an experience of regeneration later in life. The second great harm that is done is to the baby itself. It grows up with a feeling that it is safe and right in the sight of God and never repents of its sin or personally trusts Christ for eternal life. May God hasten the day when His people will do away with these man-made practices and follow the teachings of the New Testament.

Thus we have clearly seen that these ordinances were placed in the church for the purpose of commemorating Christ's broken body, shed blood, death, burial and resurrection. They are to point us back to the cross where Christ paid the supreme price for our redemption. It is a terrible thing for people, who claim to be Christ's friends, to take these ordinances and so deface them until they have no meaning whatsoever about His broken body, shed blood, or death, burial and resurrection. I believe the word of God teaches closed communion and closed baptism. Both are ordinances given to a local Baptist church. I would never think of baptizing one who is already a candidate in another Baptist church. The authority belongs to that particular local church in which the candidate has asked for baptism. In like fashion the Lord's Supper should be taken only where one holds church membership. This is "closed communion" and "closed baptism." True Baptists have always believed this great truth. Suppose I took mother's picture and decided the picture did not suit me. Suppose I said I could change that picture and make it look better. I then took a small brush and touched the picture here and there and made a mark here and there until I changed mother's picture to the point that no one would know that it was my mother's picture. For me to do such a thing would truly be an act of an ungrateful son. However, Christ left a picture of His broken body, shed blood, His death, burial and resurrection in the ordinances of the New testament Church; and His friends have been marking the picture at this place and that until the picture of Christ suffering on the cross is not recognizable. It would be far better for us to never observe the ordinance of baptism or the Lord's supper at all than to take from them their proper meaning and substitute man's conception of what these ordinances should teach.

When I come to hold the bit of unleavened bread (and I don't want it to be soda crackers but real unleavened bread, preferably prepared by the hands of a good Christian woman) and I place that emblem on my tongue, I bow my head and my mind goes back to the cross. I see the nail-pierced hands, the thorn-pierced brow, the spear-pierced side, and the scourge-gashed back of my Lord's earthly body. When I hold the little bit of the fruit of the vine and look at its redness, my mind goes back to the blood that trickled down His scourge-torn back; and I remember that this crimson flow was all for me. How can I fail to remember the price that was paid for my redemption? How can anyone substitute anything that would keep us from remembering vividly that agony that Christ endured for our souls?

Some insist that Jesus was selfish in His request to be remembered. Most everyone would like to be remembered by their loved ones. However, Jesus did not leave these ordinances in the New Testament Church for us to remember Him for His benefit. It was for our benefit. Oh, Christian, by looking back to the blood red cross our affections are kept vital and those enslaving lusts and corroding cares of this life are overcome.

Jesus could not leave all of us a material keepsake. He had only His clothes, and they were gambled for by the Roman soldiers. But Jesus did leave us something infinitely better to remember Him by and that was the picture of His fearful death with our sins upon Him. The sun is never so beautiful as it is when it comes to the death of day, when it sinks behind the blood red western clouds and hills. So Christ's life was never so beautiful, even with its deeds of love and mercy, as it was when it sank behind the blood red hill of Calvary. Oh, that gory sight, that crimson flow for our redemption! How

GREAT MONUMENTS OF THE NEW TESTAMENT CHURCH 219

can we ever forget or neglect to commemorate the ordinances that point us back to Calvary? Christ's dying request was, "Remember Calvary."

Some years ago, the United states ship, the "Maine" was blown to bits and sent to the bottom of the bay at Havana, Cuba. The United States blamed the Spanish and war was declared. At the battle of Santiago, the Commanding Officer encouraged the men and urged them on by running up a sign which read "Remember the Maine." They did remember the Maine, fought valiantly and gained a great victory during the Spanish-American war.

When Texas was warring for her independence from Mexico, Santa Anna with 5,000 Mexican soldiers attacked the Alamo at San Antonio and 186 valiant Americans fought off the Mexican hordes for many days, but at last every man of the 186 perished. They piled their bodies into a pile, poured oil over them and partially burned them. The coyotes and vultures came and picked at their bones. Meanwhile, Sam Houston was gathering an army and met Santa Anna and the Mexicans at San Jacinto and when the battle was enjoined, the cry went up "Remember the Alamo." Sam Houston gained a great victory that made Texas free from Mexico.

On December 7, 1941, Japan made a sneak attack on the United States Naval Base at Pearl Harbor. They destroyed most of our fleet there and killed over 3,000 men in that one treacherous attack. When our men started island hopping toward Japan, whether it was Guam, Iwo Jima, or Okinawa, their cry was "Remember Pearl Harbor."

Now Jesus, standing in the shadow of the cross, placed two monuments in the New Testament Church and is shouting to us across the waning centuries, through these ordinances, "Remember Calvary," "as oft as ye eat this bread and drink this cup, do it in remembrance of me." God forbid that any of us, as servants of God, could ever do anything to these monuments that would detract in any sense of the word from remembering the supreme price paid for human redemption by the Son of God, in His death on Calvary. God give us real honest-to-God Baptist preachers who will come back to the doctrines of Jesus and His Great Commission. We need a generation of Baptists with a capital "B."

CHAPTER 15

HALL OF FAME - FINAL REMARKS

The Hall of Fame - Minute Man Award

"The annual banquet for the Preacher's Hall of Fame was December 1, 1978, in Fort Worth, Texas. It was a great night. There was delicious food, outstanding entertainment, and inspiring music.

"Preachers and their wives came from far and wide to see two great men of God receive the famous Minute Man Award. The award itself is a statue of a minuteman standing on a Holy Bible cast in bronze and weighing eleven pounds. The Preacher's Hall Of Fame was founded by Dr. Jack Hall of Fort Worth, Texas, to honor great men of God while they are living. On this night, two new preachers were inducted into the Hall of Fame. These great men, Dr. Wendell Zimmerman and Dr. J.G. Tharpe, are truly worthy.

"Dr. Zimmerman is one of the original founders of the Baptist Bible Fellowship International and also of Baptist Bible College in Springfield, Missouri. He also pastored the great Kansas City Baptist Temple for many years and is now pastor of Jacksonville Baptist Temple in Florida. Dr. Zimmerman is editor of the Baptist Tribune read by people all over the world.

"Dr. Jimmy Tharpe is the beloved pastor of Baptist Tabernacle in Shreveport. Louisiana, and is founder of Baptist Christian College in the same city. It is a four-year accredited college with hundreds of students enrolled. He is in constant demand as a speaker all over America and in many foreign lands.

"These men were elected by the voting members of the Hall Of Fame. We say unto you two preachers, 'Welcome to history, gentlemen!'"

The above excerpts were taken from two newspapers on this special occasion.

Final Remarks

Some time ago I heard that my good friend, Floyd Seegers had cancer. Brother Fletcher Caldwell and I went to visit him in his home. I said, "Floyd, I'm sorry to learn that you have cancer."

I knew that Floyd was saved years ago, because I had been his pastor at Baptist Tabernacle in Sibley. I told him, "I know you're ready when the time comes." He said to me, "Jimmy, I'm packed." He assured me that he was paid up, prayed up, and ready to go. I hope, as you read this book that you are "packed" when your time comes to go. Floyd went home to be with the Lord just a few weeks ago.

At the time of the writing of this book, I have completed 47 years as pastor of Baptist Tabernacle. I have retired, passing the torch to Brother Mike Landry. And as the song says, every day with Jesus is sweeter than the day before. Every year with Baptist Tabernacle was sweeter than the year before.

I often laugh and say, "I've been in a building program for over fifty years." It seems that it has been my lot in life to build. With the church and our ministries, we have seen many precious souls come to know Christ. Many preachers were trained who are now very successful, leading some of the greatest works in America! We have graduated some very successful preachers, teachers, and businessmen and women of whom we are very proud.

It has been a good, long trip and I am thankful for every step God has allowed me to make in my ministry. I have not worried the first time about critics. I read something one day that blessed my heart. I dislike those guys who criticize and minimize vigorous guys whose enterprise rises above those guys who criticize.

Since the day I was a Methodist preacher, through the years